MW00790749

MYTHIC IMAGINATION AND THE ACTOR

In *Mythic Imagination and the Actor*, Marissa Chibás draws on over three decades of experience as a Latinx actor, writer, filmmaker, and teacher to offer an approach to acting that embraces collective imagination, archetypal work, and the mythic.

The book begins with a comparative analysis between method acting and mythic acting, encouraging actors to push past the limits of singular life experience and move to a realm where imagination and metaphor thrive. In the context of mythic acting, the book explores awareness work, solo performance creation, the power of archetypes, character building exercises, creating a body/text connection, and how to be the detective of your own process. Through this inclusive guide for a new age of diverse performers traversing gender, ability, culture, and race, readers are able to move beyond their limits to a deep engagement with the infinite possibilities of rich imagination. The final chapter empowers and motivates artists to live healthfully within the practice and create a personal artistic vision plan.

Written for actors and students of acting, American drama, and film and theater studies, *Mythic Imagination and the Actor* provides practical exercises and prompts to unlock and interpret an actor's deepest creative sources.

Marissa Chibás is a Los Angeles-based writer, filmmaker, actor, educator, and recipient of the TCG Fox Fellowship for Distinguished Achievement. She is on the Theater School faculty at California Institute of the Arts where she is Director of Duende CalArts, an initiative at CalArts Center for New Performance that produces innovative Latinx and Latin American artists. Her work as an actor has been seen on Broadway and on major stages throughout the world and her solo show, *Daughter of a Cuban Revolutionary*, has toured the U.S., Europe, and Mexico and was published by Routledge Press. For more information, visit www.marissachibas.com.

MYTHIC IMAGINATION AND THE ACTOR

Exercises, Inspiration, and Guidance
for the 21st Century Actor

Marissa Chibás

For Ariel,
May the mythic be a
guiding light on your journey.
all the best

Routledge
Taylor & Francis Group

NEW YORK AND LONDON

First published 2022
by Routledge
605 Third Avenue, New York, NY 10158

and by Routledge
2 Park Square, Milton Park, Abingdon, Oxon, OX14 4RN

Routledge is an imprint of the Taylor & Francis Group, an informa business

© 2022 Marissa Chibás

Library of Congress Cataloging-in-Publication Data
Names: Chibás, Marissa, author.
Title: Mythic imagination and the actor: exercises, inspiration, and guidance
    for the 21st century actor/Marissa Chibás.
Description: New York: Routledge, 2021. | Includes index.
Identifiers: LCCN 2021003398 (print) | LCCN 2021003399 (ebook) |
    ISBN 9780367715519 (hardback) | ISBN 9780367715502 (paperback) |
    ISBN 9781003152552 (ebook)
Subjects: LCSH: Acting.
Classification: LCC PN2061. C555 2021 (print) |
    LCC PN2061 (ebook) | DDC 792.02/8—dc23
LC record available at https://lccn.loc.gov/2021003398
LC ebook record available at https://lccn.loc.gov/2021003399

ISBN: 978-0-367-71551-9 (hbk)
ISBN: 978-0-367-71550-2 (pbk)
ISBN: 978-1-003-15255-2 (ebk)

Typeset in Joanna
by Apex CoVantage, LLC

CONTENTS

ACKNOWLEDGMENTS

I honor and am eternally grateful to the ancestors, of blood and spirit, whose stories I carry and on whose shoulders I stand. I thank the following kindred spirits: my tremendously supportive and loving husband, Travis Preston, who has always defended and protected my dreams; my kind family, especially my son, knight, and GPS, Elias Santiago Chibás Preston; the wondrous Grace Leneghan, who worked alongside me as I cobbled my proposal, edited the first draft, and was instrumental in keeping me on track to complete this book; my hermanas Ann Garcia Romero, Cynthia DeCure, Teresa Marrero, Monica Sanchez, Adriana Sevahn Nichols, and Lillian Manzour who guided my process and went above and beyond to help me reach my goal; generous Jesse Bonnell, who offered advice on an early version of the book; my chosen sister and fellow cultural warrior Dawn Saito; my dear friend and brother of my soul, Daniel Alexander Jones, who encouraged me to keep writing and whose faith in this book was the wind in my sails; and my CalArts Familia, who gave me the sabbatical that allowed me to focus time and energy on this endeavor, as well as being my creative home for over 20 years. Special thanks to former CalArts president Steven Lavine who has been a huge supporter of my work since I first joined the CalArtian community, and to all of my inspiring students—past, present and future. I am grateful to Makena

Jansen for her illustrations of the Liberator and Trickster archetypes in this book; they are far beyond what I hoped for. Thank you to my publisher at Routledge, Stacey Walker, and senior editorial assistant Lucia Accorsi, whose belief in this book and mythic imagination mean the world to me. I must end these thanks by honoring my teachers and mentors, especially George Morrison, who saw something in an open eyed 17-year-old with a thick New York City accent and introduced her to the wondrous skills and mysteries that sustain her to this day.

INTRODUCTION

This book is an articulation of what I have discovered through over three decades as an actor, writer, filmmaker, and teacher. I will share examples and exercises from my personal journey as a performer, as well as classroom insights working with students of all ages in the U.S. and abroad. In these chapters you will find the results of working with actors at some of the finest acting programs in the United States, most recently at CalArts where I currently teach in both the undergraduate and graduate acting programs. The artists I have encountered and have had the privilege to work with range from Edward Albee to Robert Wilson, from Broadway productions to a dance theater collaboration with the Florence Ballet at Brooklyn Academy of Music, from soap operas to directing my own films. This eclectic, aesthetically diverse professional experience has given me a wide breadth of approaches on how to be a 21st century actor.

You are invited to explore a different approach to acting, one that embraces the actor as a thorough, creative artist. This approach acknowledges method acting but offers a shift towards the mythic. It asks that artists leave their literal mind behind and step into the poetic and metaphorical. It posits that artists are not machines and that the creative practice is antithetical to the mechanical. The call is on another level, a mytho-poetic one.

"The Method," as it has come to be known, asks an actor to use personal memory as the core of their work. Founded on some of Stanislavski's training ideas, the Method evolved as an American variant focusing on drawing from intimate private experiences to find authenticity. Popularized by Lee Strasberg at the Actors' Studio in New York City, it became important in the post-World War II period and is particularly associated with actors such as Marlon Brando and Dustin Hoffman. With mythic acting, we are asked to push beyond the limits of our singular life experience and move to a realm where dreams and imaginations thrive. It is a way to invite poetry, mystery, and metaphor into the actor's training and everyday practice. In mythic acting, we center ourselves and release into the deep wisdom of the archetypal, rather than incorporate work that has moored itself solely to the rational.

I discovered the world of myth and its connection to acting in my early 20s through two important figures, Joseph Campbell and Clarissa Pinkola Estes. My father Raul Chibás had been a friend with Martha Graham Company principle dancer Jean Erdman for decades. They met when Raul brought Martha Graham and her company to perform in Cuba, his native country. Raul was a great modern art enthusiast, especially for modern dance. Raul and Jean rekindled their friendship when he became an exile in New York in the 1960s. Jean had a dance company of her own called The Theater of the Open Eye. I remember watching her perform at her theater when I was in college at Purchase and freshly starting my actor training. It was the late 1970s and Jean was in her 60s. She had a vibrancy and presence I had never seen before on stage. She was an inspiration to me. During the post show visit at her elegant Manhattan apartment, I briefly met her husband, Joseph Campbell, who seemed to fly in to the room and dash out with great energy and joy. It wasn't until years after meeting the extraordinary couple that I connected with Joseph Campbell's writings on myth. His book Hero of a Thousand Faces was the gateway to my mythic journey. Shortly after that I read Clarissa Pinkola Estes' seminal work Women Who Run with the Wolves. Both pieces led me to see my place in the world as a spiritual one and connected me to a long ancestral storytelling fabric that I could count on to sustain me. It was ancestral without focusing on bloodline. Myths reflect the human family, the stories that keep surfacing throughout the world and through the ages.

I was introduced to stories and ways of seeing that invited a poetic, soulful view of humanity.

This is a book you reach for when seeking replenishment and inspiration, when you need guidance and new ideas in your process. You will be led towards placing the magical and wondrous forward in your work. You will tap into creative currents and ride those waves. You will be offered ways to listen to that inner Oracle which will open pathways for you. It is often not our methodical thoughts that get us to our creative riches; rather it is listening to your wild nature. Spanish theater artist Federico García Lorca called it the Duende, that place of inspiration that is rooted in the ancient. Duende is the spirit of the earth that an artist calls forth from a deep ancestral place within, in order to give a transcendent performance. Our human story telling tradition is over 40,000 years old, as attested to by the Chauvet caves of Southern France. That lineage is powerful and full of the silt and wisdom of the age old. I will offer you exercises, prompts, and ways of seeing your work that help you deepen your imagination and relationship to your creative source.

Just as the dandelion breaks through concrete, so do our imaginations break through when superimposed with too much practicality. It is your creative force and inner soul that insists on being heard and tended to. That is the work of the artist. That is the work of the actor. Taking notice of the soul's promptings is never easy. It may move you in a direction your loved ones fear. It may mean making difficult sacrifices financially, socially, and emotionally. But the rewards are great. A calling is not safe and comfortable. The heroic journey as outlined by Joseph Campbell in his revelatory book, The Heroes Journey, begins with the hero answering the call reluctantly. This is because heroes are often happy to stay where they are; it is uncomfortable to move away from the familiar and into new territory. But answer they must and so begins a life of adventures lined with trials and rewards, the actor's journey.

How many times are actors told, "If you can do ANYTHING else, you should"? Sometimes it seems that everyone you meet needs to offer their ominous warnings about your chosen craft: "It's really a hard life" or "Very few really make it, you know." But you insist this is the road you want. "It's in my bones!" No other profession gets the kind of pessimistic response that acting does. Why? Could it be that those same people offering you council have hidden passions that have been long forgotten or buried deep within? Is your daring to follow your bliss a tremendous threat to the choices they made? Now don't get me wrong, there are frustrations and difficulties. But what profession is free of its downsides and travails? When the banking crisis of 2008 hit and so many lost their life savings, I could not help but think of those who had given up a dream, a closely held passion, in order to have financial stability. How hard it must have been for those people to wake up one day never having acted on the dream.

If you are on this path solely for stardom and living the red-carpet life, I say revisit your values. Does your soul wish to live in the land of interpreting characters, investigating texts, and helping artists realize the worlds they are building? Do you love to make believe? If you have a genuine love for this work, the work of an actor, do it. Do it with your heart and soul. No one can keep you from doing your work. You can create the space, the time, and the means to make acting your life's calling. You can construct a creative life where your various passions feed your work.

Mythic imagination is big; it is not petty. It sees the deep connection we each have to our ancient lineage. When working deeply on myself in mythic terrain, I am connecting to ancestors and stories throughout time. Mythic imagination gives you the ability to create the life you want, to seek the work and collaborators that move you, and to have the courage to put your work out there. It is so painful to hear people say, "There are too many artists and not enough work for them." I don't buy it. Artists may have an uphill battle in this society, but our culture also desperately needs artists and we have to be clever enough to place ourselves where we are needed. I will offer you some wind in the sails of your strivings, as well as practical guidance to help you grow. What else should any of us be doing other than gathering stories that need to be told and share them with the world?

Some of what I cover in this book includes awareness work, solo performance creation, the power of archetypes, character building exercises, creating a body/text connection, and how to be the detective of your own process. I hope to empower and motivate the artist in the final chapter on living healthfully within the practice and offer a guide to creating a personal artistic vision plan. I weave class exercises I teach each year at CalArts, along with personal stories and practical advice from my 35+ years as a professional actor.

The exercises and methods I use come from a multiplicity of sources and ways of working. I think an actor should be malleable. An actor must have a finely tuned instrument and be able to step in to any situation in order to serve the vision of the creators. I love actors who can trampoline themselves from theater to film to commercials to community work seamlessly and joyfully. I admire the actors who are aware that no one has the market on truth and authenticity. As our work becomes more global, an actor must know that what is seen as "real" changes from culture to culture. As a Latina, I have vivid memories of being in acting class and hearing that something I did was not "real." The wildly expressive was something I was at home with and witnessed in my Cuban household where things didn't just happen, they OCCURRED! Every director, every writer, every creator is making their vision of the world as they see it. We as actors need to go beyond our own knowledge and step into those worlds and ways of behaving laid out before us. Sometimes that means bringing in our cultural experience. Sometimes it means leaving that far behind. And so this mythic view of acting is international, makes space for an array of imaginative leanings, and does not hold one culture as the "truth" measurer.

I never subscribed to the "break them down and then build them up" actor-training model. That assumes that one's history, experiences, and past teachers are invalid and need to be erased in order to create the "real actor." That is an assembly line approach to training, too corporate, not poetic. First, insert relaxation exercise, then implant sense memory, then imprint table work, etc. adding components until the actor is built. I offer you a more circular approach. The sharp lines directly across to a certain point evaporate into circles and spirals. This approach acknowledges that *we are not machines* and we are certainly not *manufacturing a product*. It is lamentable that corporate structures and language have inundated artistic practices. Artistic expression is not like making a bar of soap where the more people like it the better it is. Artistic excellence is what to strive for, and each person you will encounter will measure that differently.

I offer ways of being as an actor that will help you move forward with your work and build a sustainable practice. What you need most is to be open and aware of what has resonated for you in your past acting work. Keep track of all you have been given through great performances you have seen, wisdom from teachers, enlightening moments in rehearsals and exercises, etc. Keep good records of all those classes, workshops, and rehearsal notes. Return to them as you need. It is like going to a well when you are thirsty. Some of the work may not resonate for you until years later. All of your experiences are there for your development. Discard nothing.

The mythic acting approach encourages you to step into your deepest self. This requires openness, discipline, curiosity, imagination, and a love of the poetic. There is nothing purely practical in the poetic. The poetic is beyond space and time. When in the reverie of the poetic, hours feel like seconds and you release yourself to surprising inner realms. I often tell my students, as my mentor George Morrison said to me, "Most of all, I want you to surprise yourself by what you can do." In order to get there, we need to let go of our plans. We need to open ourselves to wonder and embrace the creative currents stirring which are connected to that which is bigger than us. Our culture is not always open to such thoughts because they are not seen as practical. They cannot be codified. It is this arena we must boldly plunge ourselves into as artists and turn away from the mocking voices within and without. We must ask ourselves, "What stirs my soul?" That is the portal to your creative depth. That is where mythic imagination lives.

There is no question that there are also practical elements in addition to the poetic in this book. I was deeply heartened by an event at the Los Angeles CalArts Theater known as REDCAT, where the great actor and CalArts alum Don Cheadle spoke about his process. When the interviewer asked him about preparing for roles with "actions and objectives" he turned to her and said that he did not work in that way. He said he worked with a Jungian analyst within his dreams. I just about jumped out of my seat for joy. It was wonderful to hear such a powerful voice in film, theater, and television credit dream work as a way of reaching his inspiring performances.

I offer you ways of seeing your journey as an actor from a mythic perspective, aligning you with history's storytellers. I hope that learning the old stories and archetypes of acting is both empowering and inspiring for you. Acting is a truly ancient and noble art. Keep yourself open. If you can make believe, you can act. Our work is about authentically and completely allowing our imaginations to run free, like children on a playground. And so, let us begin this wondrous hero's journey together and play.

1

THE MYTHIC SENSE

Mytho-Poetic Mind

To start, let me introduce what it means to see things from the mythic rather than the literal sense. Once we have a grasp of this, we can move on to our exercises in a way that leaves behind what many of us have experienced as "learning" in favor of education. To "educate" means "to bring forward," so this mythic approach acknowledges that rather than cramming you with information, the process in this book lays out a kind of "remembering." That is how I like to teach, serving as a guide that brings forward knowledge inherent in each student. The literal mind focuses on facts, questions the poetic, and cannot grasp metaphor. And without metaphor, there is no poetry, no music, no art, no great actor.

The mythic is tied to the collective human story, that which inspires and grounds us as individuals while connecting us to what is age old. Myths speak to our deepest dreams, fears, and wisdoms. Although the mythic is with us every day it is often ignored in our busy and sometimes soul crushing modern lives. When we access the mythic, we are aligned with our true nature and that which stirs deeply in us and to our soul's purpose. Myths are great stories that serve as guides for us to better understand our experience of humanity. They are stories that stand the test of time because they speak profoundly through metaphor. Just as the great teachers throughout history have used parables and kōans to lead people to a deeper understanding of human experience, so too do myths through metaphor and symbols. In my work with actors, I seek to mine the mythic that is stirring in them in order to connect their work to that deeper purpose. Metaphor is key to connecting to the mythic.

It is impossible to approach Hamlet's "To be or not to be" speech from a literal mind. The entire speech centers on metaphor to contemplate existence vs. non-existence. As actors we do ourselves a great disservice trying to understand texts from the literal. Allow yourself genuine reflection that invites twists and turns. Resist being the actor who simply wants the answer behind a text. Instead be the one who engages and dances with that text mytho-poetically and finds the mythic to release you from the literal.

The mythic approach acknowledges that we as artists have a poetic purpose and that we are all on a hero's journey. My process as a teacher includes teaching skills for the art of acting as well as helping actors connect to that purpose. Too many of us actors go along for years without ever asking essential questions: What am I passionate about? What stories do I need to tell? Who is doing the work I am drawn to, and how do I connect with that work? We are propelled by the machine of an industry that rarely bothers to notice their audience except on the crudest level of product information gathering. We run along our busy lives, out of breath, barely able to consider who we really are. I challenge you to take time as you read these pages to reflect on what is stirring within you that you may not be paying attention to. What is your oracle trying to alert you to and how can you respond? At the end of this chapter is an exercise for you to awaken that inner oracle.

Joseph Campbell envisaged that the refusal of the call is one of the first steps on the "hero's journey." There is a good reason for that. Many of the things our soul guides us toward are uncomfortable. Perhaps that calling uproots us from those we love, or changes the image our loved ones have of us. Perhaps the call requires resources we do not feel we possess. I have often felt myself reluctantly answering a call and putting off a more financially lucrative idea. I have learned that the call does not go away and can come back with greater force and determination or manifest itself in destructive behavior, even illness, if ignored. One thing is certain. Although it can sometimes be difficult, answering the call is what our soul needs. Remember we are not material beings having an occasional spiritual experience but spiritual beings having an occasional material one. Much of life's suffering comes from inverting those two ideas.

And so, the mythic asks us to turn in and contemplate, not just seek the easy answers that are fed to us. The reflection of a great text, image, music, etc. takes us to inner realms and wanderings, a kind of soulful pilgrimage.

The Dung Beetle

I like to share with my students the true story of the dung beetle. The dung beetle, also known as the scarab, is a sacred creature for the Ancient Egyptians that navigates its path on the earth by following the Milky Way. Scientific studies have found that when the dung beetle is put in a dark room with a different constellation overhead, the beetle gets lost and wanders aimlessly. When the Milky Way is reproduced above, it finds its course again. How can something so small be guided by something so large? How can the tiny beetle feel the pattern of the universe? How can we invite a similar navigation?

Elegua

Before we begin our journey together, let us turn to the Yoruban deity who opens pathways, Elegua. This deity is one of the Orishas, who came from the spirit world and then shape shifted into human form here on Earth. The Orishas' stories, songs, and religion were carried to the Americas by people enslaved from West Africa. Elegua is represented as both an old man and a mischievous child, a wonderful playful paradox! He is the Lord of the Crossroads and a threshold guardian. His colors are red and black. It is through Elegua that humans can communicate with the other

Orishas. In Cuba, where my ancestors are from, each Orisha has a Catholic counterpart. Elegua's Catholic counterpart is Saint Anthony, the guardian of children. And so, we open ourselves to Elegua and ask him his blessing as we embark on our path together.

The Story of Lailah

In order to align with that mythic sense, we need to remember something that the Jewish tale of the angel Lailah reminds us. Before you were born, your soul was ripening on the branch of the Tree of Life. I like to imagine this tree as the sacred Ceiba tree of the Caribbean. This tree has roots that extend for miles and it is said that the souls of our ancestors exist in those roots. When a soul is fully ripe, the angel Gabriel takes the soul from the branch and carries it to Lailah, who in turn plants the soul in the womb of the mother. Just before birth, Lailah lights a candle on the forehead of the unborn child and illuminates their entire life before them. The child is able to see its life path and purpose. Then, as the child is born Lailah blows out the candle and presses her index finger to that spot just above the lip of the newborn and whispers, "Shhh." The child then can no longer see the path that a moment before Lailah had revealed. If you place your finger on that spot above your lip and under your nose, you can feel the indentation of where Lailah pressed her finger. That is why when we are deep in thought, we often touch this part of our face as if remembering something essential, connecting ourselves to that soul's journey. Let us now tune in and see if we can realign with what Lailah once illuminated.

Turning In and Listening

The Oxford English Dictionary defines an oracle as "a priest or priestess acting as a medium through whom advice or prophecy was sought from the gods in classical antiquity." In the yearly Greek initiation known as the Eleusinian mysteries with roots in pre-Greek Minoan Crete, participants went through a series of rites and ended their journey in front of a priestess who was the "Oracle." That Oracle gave them the knowledge and guidance they needed to continue on their path. Many ancient Greek plays end with the Oracle deciding the fate of the characters on stage. It is the Oracle that leads humans to truth, no matter how painful or joyful.

George Morrison led his acting class through many guided meditations that helped his students rely on those inner Oracles and voices the imagination sends us. It was always extraordinary to me the surprising visits these guided meditations led me to. I found myself embedded in memories that emerged to help me answer questions and offer knowledge and advice. Taking time to tune in and turn towards those inner promptings is essential for the actor. It is also important to allow for the surprises. Our gold is in what the imagination chooses to bring forth, which is always connected to the unconscious, to our dream state. This means surrendering and allowing for the idiosyncratic to emerge. You do not have to try to make this happen. It will come. The floodgates open when the imagination is invited in. Getting the body, mind, and spirit ready for the imagination takes just a little bit of time and focus.

Here is a Centering Exercise I have learned that can be done before each exercise in this book. There are many versions of this so feel free to adjust, as you need to. We will follow right after centering with the Oracle Exercise. It is valuable to hear the words of the exercise guide you. Have someone read to you the steps or record yourself reading the exercises before you dive in. Have pen and paper ready beside you to jot down anything that speaks to you. Later in the book there is a chapter on personal artistic visioning that can guide you to realizing some of the things your inner Oracle reveals to you. These revelations can be used while working on a role, while creating your own project, or to find deeper meaning in a text. When we open up and invite wisdom in, the deeper parts of ourselves come forward and take charge.

Centering Exercise

I invite you to breathe and take a moment right now to set the reading down, close your eyes.

Sit on a chair where you can feel your sitz bones making contact. Allow yourself to have an elongated spine. Feel your shoulder blades connected to your back, where your wings are. Imagine those wings expanding wide. Feel your heart center, the breastbone area, open and free. Let your neck be free. Feel your head bobbing easily at the top of your spine. Relax your jaw. Relax your face. Breathe. Breathe. Notice your breath as it travels in and out of your body with ease. What do you feel expand on the inhalation, what do you feel on the exhalation? Breathe. Take a few minutes just noticing your breath with ease.

Now expand that awareness to the sensation of your heart beating and your blood pulsing throughout your body. Nice and easy. Effortless. Keep the breath free, jaw and face relaxed.

Now imagine yourself at the top of a mountain or building. You are safe there. You are perfectly balanced in space. You are perfectly balanced in space.

Take a moment now to connect with that which you are most passionate about. Maybe it is a person or a place or an idea. Whatever it is, take a moment to connect with that which you are most passionate about. Where does that live in your body? What stirs and awakens, and where do you sense that stirring when you connect with that which you are most passionate about? Breathe. Nice and easy. No effort.

Now send what you are most passionate about throughout your body and radiate it 360 degrees around you, so that the other objects in the room, the very walls and beyond are now affected by what you are passionate about. Take a few minutes to be in this connected state. Open your eyes when you are ready. Take in the room; take in others in the room. You are now centered and ready for your practice.

Oracle Exercise

Find a quiet area that is a place of refuge for you. It can be in your home or in nature. Be sure you can feel at ease and without people peering at you. Have your journal nearby. Go ahead and create an invitation to the Oracle. It can be as simple as closing your eyes and saying, "I invite you, Oracle, to come and speak to me." It can also be more involved. Perhaps you want to create an altar and offer at that altar something in particular for the Oracle. You can think of your altar as something like backstage dressing room spaces. It is always fascinating to see how we actors use those little squares of table and light given to us to get ready before our shows. Notice what you tend to place around you. Perhaps a picture of a loved one, or the playwright, or an image that is related to the play you are doing. That is an altar of sorts. Start with that idea and see where it takes you. Once you have invited the Oracle, close your eyes and breathe deeply. Give yourself time to listen, don't just hear. When you are ready, open your eyes and write down what the Oracle offered you. If you came up blank or don't trust what you heard, try again. It may take some time for you to open yourself up to this kind of practice. Remember we get better at what we practice.

When you have completed this exercise take a moment to write in your journal. It is best to feel free when you write and to know that this is something just for you, no need to share with anyone. So, go ahead and make grammatical errors, exclaim, and let yourself go. Put pen to page and write from your heart and soul. Let the images flow. Take a moment to read what you have written and take the words in. Notice any surprises, ideas, etc. that jump out at you. See if there is anything from this exercise that you'd like to put in to further practice.

These exercises will open the pathway to our deepest creativity and mythic sense. There is no way of muscling ourselves through that. We need to work towards being an open and receptive channel. When you get in that practice, new inner terrain opens up and you will be surprised by the messages and promptings you receive. Many studies have been done that prove that our most creative time is not when we are "trying" to problem solve, but during walks, taking a shower, or other moments that let our minds and spirits wander. Let us embrace that wanderlust and see where our imaginations take us.

2

LAYING THE GROUND WORK

First Steps

When leading my actors or students, I find it is important to begin with a foundation of agreements in terms of communication among the group in order to make the space conducive to creativity. To work freely in that *"safely, bravely and with abandon"* place, we need to agree on what we expect of ourselves and of others. I take three large sheets of white drawing paper and tape them up on a wall of the studio. I write at the top of each sheet the following questions—

What is great acting?
What is performance?
What do I expect of others and myself?

Then with different colored markers on the floor, I ask two volunteers from the group to act as scribes, writing the words that are being shouted out onto these sheets. I let the volunteers know that they can put the words in any direction and with whatever flair they choose. We start with "What is great acting?" The actors in the room share what comes to mind: believing, discipline, versatility, imagination, risk, joy, play, etc. When the page is full of colored words, you move on to the next one, and so on for the third.

This last question is crucial. The group has thus far explored what great acting and performance means to them. They inspire each other with the words they are sharing. It is wonderful to hear the recognition in their voices when a word is shared that they all agree is important. Once the group arrives at the last question, they realize that to become the performers they want to be, with the elements that they named, they must come together as a collective and hold each other accountable with their behavior and discipline. Here we experience a public recognition of the behavior we need in the studio to achieve excellence.

At the end of this process they break into groups, roughly four or five actors per group. Each participant picks three words from each list, for a total of nine words per person. In their small group, they then share the words they chose and begin to craft three sentences that encompass as many of those chosen words as possible. The result is an affirmation that the group has reached through reflection and dialogue. I encourage all participants to contribute to the final three sentences and for everyone to make sure all have had a voice in the process. It is common for someone to want to take the lead and write out the entire affirmation. I ask that the groups be mindful and sensitive to bringing the quieter voices in and including them.

Once each group is done with their three-sentence affirmation, they are read aloud to the entire group and are put together to make a single mission statement for that class or workshop. In addition I like to share my expectations that they must bring to the work, including mutual respect, an appreciation of differences, discipline, kindness, and imagination. When the missions are read out loud, the artists come together and raise the bar for each other in the present moment. They are then able to hold themselves and each other accountable. The group missions I have witnessed throughout the years are unique expressions of that particular group and are snapshots into their creative collective soul.

Now we have laid the groundwork to be able to work together. We have created a collective mission statement that we each sign, including the workshop leader, and commit to upholding. When issues arise we can go to the mission statement and make clear the expectations that were set by the group. Sometimes just a word reminder can bring the class back to focus and intent if it has veered away from the mission. Here is an example of a mission statement created in one of my first year MFA Acting classes:

> It is our 100% commitment to maintain a safe space for the development of theater and performance from all backgrounds. We pride ourselves in the ability to connect, collaborate, and create openly and professionally. We value our uninhibited imaginations to prompt us in leaving no stone unturned and to trust in the process.
>
> We are a coven of mythical, magical, nice demons. Our mission is to surrender our light with the dedication to create transcendent worlds for everyone. We believe these worlds organically inspire joy and connection.
>
> Ingredients: The pantry of a well-fed actor is incomplete without the main ingredients of truth, vulnerability, connection, openness, and imagination. To enhance the flavor, you must add a dash of commitment and a few sprigs of curiosity. These ingredients cannot be added haphazardly: They must be cooked with discipline, and joy of work, left to simmer over a lifetime. If you don't like the taste you must spit it out; you must be honest, unapologetic and willing to fail, in order for Theatre to nourish you.
>
> We are cultivating relationships and overcoming adversity through unity and empathy. It is through open communication, trust, and vulnerability that we can achieve this radical unity despite physical limitations.

Getting Up on Our Feet, in Our Bodies and Voices

The first exercise I lead with any group of actors I am working with is an Awareness Exercise that I learned from George Morrison, my undergraduate teacher and beloved mentor. We cannot move forward as actors if we are unaware of what we are doing. Progress begins with awareness. That is different than self-consciousness. When we are self-conscious, we are in judgment of what we are aware of. A good actor is able to simply, without judgment, be aware of what their bodies, voices, etc. are doing in space and adjust as needed. The Awareness Exercise is the actor version of the ballet plié. It all starts there. The following exercise is done in a group but can be modified for someone working on their own.

Please begin with the Centering Exercise in Chapter 1.

Awareness Exercise

Place yourselves around the room with plenty of space between you. Choose someone to be outside of the group who can start and stop the exercise. At the same time all participants will walk around the room and with a full voice say out loud "I am aware of ___." Your awarenesses should be simply what you see around you, no interpreting, as well as sensations you are feeling. For example, "I am aware of the light of the sun coming in to the room. I am aware of an itch in my right ear. I am aware of feeling nervous. I am aware that you just smiled at me. I am aware of the white tape hanging from the board . . . etc." All this is happening as you all speak at the same time and move about the room. It is important to have awarenesses both in the room as well as sensations and feelings that you are experiencing. One thing that is essential is that you have sensitivity in this, and all group exercises, of what you choose to share. If you are beginning a collaboration and you see someone in the room and say, "I am aware of your crooked teeth," it's not the best way to start that partnership. So be aware and be free, but with sensitivity to yourself and others. I like to say to students with these exercises to move "safely, bravely, and with abandon." Yes, we can do all that.

Pause after a few minutes. Close your eyes and be aware of what just happened. What did you notice? How did that feel? Were you mostly aware of externals or internals? Did you move freely from one awareness to the next, or did you stop yourself in some way? Did you speak full voice or were you hiding? You will see how many awarenesses came into consciousness and how much is going on every millisecond. You heard others voicing awarenesses while you were articulating your own. So much is going on at the same time! That's what it is like for us on stage, but we are not usually aware of just how much is happening simultaneously. Our work is very similar to the professional athlete competing. Multiple awarenesses are needed to reach our goals.

Please check in and make sure the words are simply "I am aware of . . ." Some actors change this to "I am aware of the fact that. . .," or other versions. It's important to keep it simple. Sometimes actors feel the need to "perform" this exercise and add things like "I am aware of feeling hungry and I realize that back in my dorm I have a ham sandwich that I'd love to have a bite of right now . . ." All you need for this exercise is the first part, "I am aware of feeling hungry." The rest is an avoidance of the present moment. Practicing being unapologetically in the present moment as an actor is essential. This is a terrific exercise to get in touch with those inner obstacles that tell us we are not enough and that we need to do more to be interesting. Doing the Awareness Exercise simply and directly gets us to confront those inner critics, and leave them in the dust. The great news is that awareness is halfway to solving whatever it is we are working on. Just being aware of the tension in my neck helps me to release the tension in my neck. It takes a bit of time, but that is the process. The more aware we are, the more we are able to shift to become a free, open, and imaginative instrument. The Awareness Exercise is the first step in getting us there. Each of these exercises that we do is a microcosm of what we are doing on stage or on screen as actors. If you found yourself rushing through the exercise, chances are that you tend to rush on stage. Awareness of rushing will bring us to rushing less and less. That's how this works. As soon as you are aware, something inside you begins to adjust. With effortless ease you will see the positive changes you can make practicing this very simple and essential exercise. Make this your plié, your touchstone.

Additions to Awareness Exercise

Find a partner and speak simultaneously as you continue to be aware. This time allow each other's awarenesses to affect you. Perhaps one of you is aware of wanting to jump; the other hears that and begins to jump. You then may find yourselves following through on impulses motivated by the awareness. This can be a very exuberant part of the exercise, a place where you and your partner play "safely, bravely, with abandon" together. It is important to be aware of the other participants in the room as you do this. They can be included as well. The vision can expand and open up from tunnel vision. Take it all in, including your own feelings and kinesthetic sensations. Later on when we get to scene work there is an addition to this exercise that is excellent for partner connection and finding character motivations in a scene. You will find that exercise in the character building skills section.

Once finished with this latest exercise, close your eyes again and check in. How did that feel? Did it differ from the first Awareness Exercise? Any new discoveries? Use your journal to jot down your observations.

Sensorily Grounded Language

With all the work we do it is important to use *sensorily grounded language* when talking about it. For example, if you finish an exercise and say, "I felt weird," there is not much we can learn from that. What is the sensorily grounded language that articulates "weird" for you? Maybe it is a tingly sensation in the chest or tightness in the throat. Once you have that language, then you can do something with it, as opposed to "weird" which is outside of the actual experience. We need to get directly into what we are experiencing.

Here is an example of how we can use sensorily grounded language. Sayda is a first year MFA Acting student and just did the Awareness Exercise for the first time.

MARISSA: Any observations? How did that go?

SAYDA: That was really fun.

MARISSA: Great. What is fun? What is that in sensorily grounded language?

SAYDA: I don't know . . . just fun.

MARISSA: Yes, but how does that particular kind of fun feel? What was going on in your body, your spirit?

SAYDA: I felt . . . I don't know . . . free.

MARISSA: What does "free" feel like? Is that somewhere in your body? Is there an image or sensation that comes to you?

SAYDA: (*begins to move her hands around her shoulder area*) I don't know, it kind of feels free up here, around my shoulders. I felt like I was flying. Like I was a kid in a playground again.

MARISSA: Great. Yes, that is sensorily grounded language. That gesture you used with your hands around your shoulders is sensorily grounded.

It lets me know specifically where your body felt "fun" and "free." Now you know what free is, at least with this exercise. Your body knows what that is and where it is located, so you can go there again when you want to.

Sayda started with a general observation that became very specific, specific for her. Someone else may feel fun located somewhere else in the body. It is this specificity that we as actors need to draw from and bring to our roles. The sensorily articulated is what gives our characters their specificity, their detail, and their fully alive three-dimensionality.

Creating Sacred Space

No matter where an actor works, the space they engage with needs to become sacred. Especially as rehearsal processes get more and more corporate, we need to find ways to remind ourselves of the spiritual aspect of what we do, no matter how dreary a space we may be in. There is always something to fall in love with. Actors are some fabulous complainers. We can be in the most incredible setting and find cause to complain. We are also great lovers. Falling in love with our space is as important as anything we do as actors. It is a form of alchemy, of magic, and it is one of our actor essentials.

The Taínos, the first people of the land known now as the Caribbean, believed that people and nature were created out of rays of sun. Look around at your collaborators and see them each as rays of sun. Look around and see your space as something the rays of the sun created. Already the space has transformed.

> O lovers, lovers it is time
> to set out from the world.
> I hear a drum in my soul's ear
> coming from the depths of the stars.
> —Rumi

I learned the following ritual and adapted it from chorographer/director Mirah Love. I use this at the initiation of any group I am working with.

Falling in Love With Your Space Exercise

Please begin with the Centering Exercise in Chapter 1, only without the chair. Please do this version standing so you have a clear open space around you. Each participant will walk around the room and fall in love with something that is particular to the space itself: a piece of tape on the floor, a cord hanging from the ceiling, a chair, etc. Just as love in life, you need to take a little time. At first you may be drawn to that blue paint on the wall, but after spending time with it you realize that it is not your true love. Go ahead and leave that bit of paint and keep looking. Once you have found that love, the true one that calls you, spend some time with it. Notice all the details of your love. Appreciate it more and more, letting yourself fall deeper and deeper in love. You may move with your love, or simply just observe, but learn and notice all you can about your love.

All participants are doing this at the same time. Occasionally, two participants fall in love with the same part of the room. That's okay; the room won't mind the attention. After a few minutes with your love, come back together. Then each participant will take everyone to their love to introduce their love to the class. They will each say just a few things about their love. There is a second part to this potentially that is shared in the monologue chapter. Here is an example of a student engaging with this exercise:

CARTER: (*He takes us to a broken piano pedal in the corner of the studio. He hunches down below the piano and angles his body so he can be near the pedal, but so as the class can see it too. He slowly reaches for the pedal but doesn't touch it.*) My love is a bit shy. He's been through a lot. It took me a while to get him to warm up to me. He's been lied to before. But he likes it when I am here next to him. Please keep a bit of distance, ok? (*The others agree and take a small step back.*) I took my time and, well, as you can see he is injured. (*He lifts the injured pedal up a bit, very gently.*) I let him know one of the things I love about him is that he's still brassy and shiny, I think he is real cute. I love that he may be a little broken but he still can make the piano sound better. He's the finishing touch. I love that he is strong and capable, no matter what it seems like. I love how shiny he is. Oh, and his name is Kevin. Thank you. (*The participants clap and another participant guides the others to their love.*)

This exercise often reveals much about the person sharing. It tends to open up even the most seemingly tough folks. It is a very moving exercise and a real heart opener, which is a big part of the intention. It is also a fun way to appreciate and get to know each other. At the end of this exercise the room is transformed. A room turns sacred; it is made sacred by those who choose to see the beauty in even the roughest of details. If you can fall in love with a light switch, a torn carpet, ragged wallpaper, or a broken piano pedal, you can certainly fall in love with that which your character loves, especially another person. All the stories we tell include something that our characters would live and die for, and this exercise not only gets us to see how we can magically make the dreary special, it lets us know the power of our willingness to open our hearts. If you can open your heart to a space, you can do that with others, with ideas, with objects, etc. Many have been surprised by the emotional connection they experience when sharing the story of their love. This love is in essence the thing we take for granted daily. This is one of the purposes of our craft: to make sacred the ordinary, to bring the discarded or undervalued to light.

Ritual of Engagement and Disengagement

In order to maintain a healthy and sustainable practice, we need to make sure we are entering our work through a clear and conscious threshold and leaving it with the same. Many acting teachers talk about the importance of preparation to enter a scene or monologue; I like to use rituals of engagement and rituals of disengagement. A ritual of engagement is essentially some kind of process you give yourself to enter a role. It can include movement, sound, and/or objects. It can change from role to role so that you respond to that particular character's needs. Perhaps you play some music and slowly put on a hat that brings you in to the role. The ritual of disengagement is similar to the preceding and is the exit of the role done prescriptively. I worked with an actor who would take an imaginary mask off his face and say, "That's done" as his ritual of disengagement. This process allows the actor to invite their imagination to drive them while stepping in and out of character. The ritual part of it takes your work away from the quotidian, acknowledging that you are doing something special and out of the ordinary. It is something like walking into the magic wardrobe and then inevitably coming out. The actor enters into the world of the character, and then must leave that all behind.

Rituals of engagement and disengagement offer the actor clear moments that help them step away from the problems and woes of the characters they are playing. Many actors know the issues of carrying the vulnerabilities, aggressions, or other behaviors home with them, only to create chaos for loved ones or even to strangers. The tabloids are filled with stories of actors unable or unwilling to create the necessary boundaries for their own sake as well as for those they love. I say keep the drama on the stage or screen. These rituals will delineate those lines for you. Whatever you create for yourself will work as long as you commit fully to it. Remember in this process, as with all we do, follow the body's lead.

Improvs

Now you are ready to do a Contact Improv Exercise. You have connected first with your breath and body, then with the space, then with a partner. You will now extend that and connect with the room and those around you. I learned this Contact Improv Exercise from working with the late Seattle-based choreographer, Della Davidson. I was very fortunate to have worked with her at the Sundance Theater Lab in 2008. I like to share with my students the Mary Oliver quote, "Let the soft animal in your body love what it loves." This following of that soft yet animalistic feeling is where we want to be as performers.

The Body Leads

It is important to place focus on letting the body lead and to move from pleasure, rather than move in ways you think you "should" or is "correct." In order to do this, we need to spiral into relishing the kinesthetic place. That is the place that Mary Oliver is referring to in her quote. It means to turn in towards that primal connection, fully awake and aware, listening to your surroundings and internal impulses. This is the state of play that you see children accessing in playgrounds. It is that joyful kinesthetic abandon we invite naturally as children and need to relearn as adults. I used to love watching my son leap on to the monkey bars and fly in space when he was little. He was graceful, fully aware of his surroundings, and deeply connected to his body's movements all at the same time. He just knew what he could or could not do, and he took physical risks with focus and determination. This childlike openness and daring is very important for Contact Improv.

Soft Focus

Practice soft focus first on your own, then with the group you are working with. In order to move in the space and be free, you need to access a focus that allows you to see everything without focusing on a single thing. That is soft focus. Of course you can at times directly look at others in the space, but for the most part the soft focus will enable you to feel the space around you and to take in as much of what is going on in the room as possible. Narrow or direct focus is limiting. Here is an exercise that will help you develop soft focus.

Put your index finger in front of your face, about a foot away. Look at your finger. Now change your focus to look at the space beyond your finger and all around it. Take in as much of the space as you can. Now go back to directly looking at the finger. Now back to the space beyond it. Has it expanded at all? With practice it will. Expanding your soft focus is a great and important tool for the actor.

Further Exploration on Soft Focus

Place your index finger in front of you. Move it horizontally towards your left temple while keeping your focus center, as if the finger were still there. Keep an eye on the finger as long as you can before it goes naturally to soft focus. Now practice this to the right. This is adapted from a yoga exercise and helps with our peripheral vision.

When working on these exercises, be sure to keep connecting back to that joyful childlike playfulness. Keep yourself free and easy. Make sure to check in to see if your:

Neck is free
Jaw is relaxed
Forehead is relaxed

Breath is free
The bottoms of your feet are grounded into the floor

What's in the Room? Exercise

Move around the room and take the temperature. Do a little inventory of your body, those around you, in the space. What's in the room? What impulses are waiting to come to the fore in your body and with others? Be sure to listen to where your body leads, as well as be affected by others' impulses. Allow yourself to shift on a dime and respond to your impulse to try something new. If you start out moving slow, change the dynamic. This is all done with 360-degree awareness to be sure you and your partners are safe. Move in ways that feel good in your body.

Begin to walk and run in the space. Explore the parts of the room that may be lonely, need a body to fill them. Notice what others are doing and respond by joining them or moving in opposition. Begin to find a physical conversation between you, others in the space, and the room. Everything is alive. Step fully into that aliveness safely and with abandon. Stay present and in the room. Use that soft focus. Listen with your whole body.

Continue the exercise and add, a step at a time, the following movement explorations:

Walk
Run
Sit
Stand
Push
Pull
Spiral
Hold

With each addition keep the exploration as pure as possible. This does not need to look any particular way. Allow yourself to explore levels, pace, quality of movement, speed, etc. By now you are exploring all of the above at the same time and the room is alive between you and your partners. You continue to open yourselves to each other and the space.

This is a particularly good sequence for coming together as a group. It is a way of discovering ensemble. I added to Della's list of movement exploration the "spiral." It came out of doing a hip opening exercise with a group of MFA actors. Afterwards, the students were sharing their experiences. One young man said he really appreciated the spiraling part of the exercise. He articulated that so many of the Contact Improvs and ways of moving were angular and focused on horizontal and vertical type movements. A light bulb went off for me. In most contemporary movement explorations, the feminine archetypal movement of the circle and the spiral is left out. For that reason I began looking for that quality of movement in other exercises as well. In my experience, there is a deep need for exploring what we are not habitually experiencing in our daily lives. The body calls out for it and recognizes what it is missing, as it did for this young actor.

After this sequence you are centered on your breath, you are aligned in your body, and you are awakened to your awarenesses. You are now ready to work.

Guidance for Improv Work

When leading exercises like this, it is necessary to offer language that encourages the participants to build on their new freedom. I call out, along with the movement directives, encouragements such as:

Change your impulse on a dime.
If you find yourself staying in a certain tempo or way of moving, change that.
Respond to the impulses in yourself and the room.
What does your body feel like doing through this exploration?
Move in ways that feel pleasurable.
Free yourself up, let loose.
Safely, bravely, with abandon.

In a later chapter, I will share exercises for spoken improvs.

3

ARCHETYPES

The Mythic Within Me

I was a professional flower girl. Nearly once every month, from the time I was 4 until about 9, I was the first to walk down a ruby red carpet of a beautifully ornate and cavernous church. I remember the almost paralyzing terror of being completely alone, my white patent leather shoes shifting nervously below me.

I am in the middle of the ocean with no way to reach solid ground. I hold my breath and my body tightens. Far behind me is the wedding party; I can't count on them for help. I feel everyone watching me from the pews and am terrified to make a mistake. The giant altar seems a universe away and reaching it feels like it will take days. How did I get here? How do I do this? I turn to look at the onlookers whose faces encourage me to continue on. The organ music begins to play. Everything seems suspended, as if the world were holding its breath, waiting for the bride hidden behind me to be revealed. It is up to me to open the space for that entrance. I take a deep breath and realize I have no choice but to move forward. I take the first step. That's when something shifts inside me, softens. I submit.

At that moment I gave in to the greatness of the task and stepped into my role. The music carried me along and I found more ease with each step. That is one of my earliest memories of being taken by the mythic. I was not just a young child named Marissa walking alone down a terribly long and imposing aisle, but *The Flower Girl* preparing a sacred space for the bride. Something seemed to hold me up and guide my hand to the basket to scatter the white petals along the pathway. It was a feeling of the power of community and fulfilling ritual. I stepped into a solemnity of space. A moment before, I had been joking and goofing off with the bridesmaids, but now there was no room for that. The air was thick and charged with the weight of this moment. Something was expected of me, something age old. I had a purpose. I stepped into mythic terrain.

This was the humble start to a lifelong commitment to acting. It is interesting that only recently, when I set out to write this acting book, have I recalled my flower girl past. Before when asked when I began acting I would refer to an early elementary school play. Yet, as I began this book the images of those flower girl memories overtook me. I know that those epic moments in my early life served as an initiation of the deep connection between performance and the mythic. It was the archetype of The Flower Girl that I stepped into and that carried me beyond my fears.

Archetypes are a very powerful way for actors to align with the mytho-poetic in their work and to discover depths in characterizations. Time and time again my students have expressed that their work on archetypes opened universes for them.

Archetypes

An archetype is the opposite of a stereotype. A stereotype seeks to diminish or limit with generalizations and projected prejudices. An archetype is universal, limitless, and not constrained to the temporal or reductive. The hero archetype can be of any age, of any culture, and any race or ethnicity. We see these archetypes in stories throughout the world and throughout time. When an actor steps into an archetype, say, *The Trickster*, they are leaning on a powerful figure whose memory exists in the very bones of the performer. To step into The Trickster means to be calling on an ancient collective memory, not just what one has personally experienced. The writer Robert Johnson calls archetypes a manifestation of a collective dream of people and the writer Maureen Murdock sees archetypes as recurring patterns of human behavior.

Archetypes are fluid, not fixed; they are powerful portals to finding the specificity and dynamism of the characters we are portraying. The archetype you are exploring is in constant flux and lives in an original way within your body and therefore can be completely different in someone else. So, there is no *correct* way to step into a given archetype, yet it is recognizable to others when you have authentically moved into your version of that archetype. Because these archetypes are personas that have been around for thousands of years, and have been developed, expanded, and brought forward in stories for ages, they are known to us on a cellular level. The process of exploring these archetypes is akin to remembering, to allowing the body to take us to what it inherently knows.

Psychoanalyst and artist Carl Jung created the concept of the archetypal. His work has been an influence on countless writers including Joseph Campbell and Robert Johnson. Johnson's book *Owning Your Own Shadow* has been in my acting class curriculum for over a decade. I highly recommend exploring the works of these writers, as well as that of Marion Woodman and Maureen Murdoch.

I led a workshop with a group of teenagers who were recent arrivals from Central America seeking refuge in the United States. This workshop focused on stepping into the body of a hero/heroine. I had been witnessing the effect of the negative rhetoric about immigrants during the 2016 presidential campaign and wanted to offer something to counteract that negativity. I could see, even just driving around my neighborhood in Los Angeles, the way the slumped bodies of young Latinos were expressing shame and demoralization. I conducted the workshop at various high schools and community centers along with the team of *Shelter*, a play on the subject of these young migrants we produced with the CalArts Center for New Performance/Duende CalArts. After first leading them in some fun theater games to warm up the group, as well as the Centering Exercise from the first chapter, we began.

Stepping Into Hero Archetype Exercise

Now that you are centered, take a moment to bring to mind a hero, some-one you know, of any gender or non-binary disposition. They can be from this time period or any time past. Take a moment to choose someone you truly admire, whose actions are an inspiration to you.

Once they have chosen that hero, I pull out *Actor Archetype Cards*. They are much like a deck of playing cards, but with images and descriptions of 80 archetypes. The students are immediately drawn to the cards, as if

Figure 3.1 The Trickster
Source: Illustrated by Makena Janssen

something in them instantly recognized their power. These cards often transfix my students, satisfying a creative thirst. They often have a hard time choosing just one card/archetype to work with. Luckily, they can always go to the deck and play with a different archetype whenever they want. It is always a treat for me to see their imaginations get ignited through this simple yet dynamic offering. Here is an example of The Trickster:

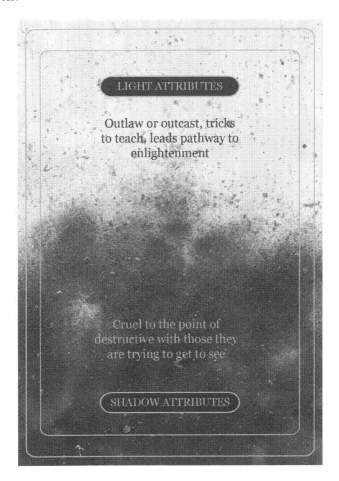

Figure 3.2 Light attributes: outlaw or outcast, tricks to teach, leads pathway to enlightenment. Shadow attributes: cruel to the point of destructive with those they are trying to get to see

Source: Illustrated by Makena Janssen

Imagine what archetype the hero you have chosen embodies. Perhaps your hero has many archetypes within them. Choose one to work with for the moment. The cards have an image of the archetype on one side along with a description of its light and shadow attributes on the other side.

First focus on the light aspect of the archetype you chose. Look at the image on the card. Let it speak to you. What do you notice? Keeping in mind this light attribute of the archetype of your hero, find a gesture or movement in your body that expresses their essence. Go ahead and step into a gesture that truly feels what that archetype is about. Take all the space you need. Use your whole body freely. Make sure as you do the gesture or physical movement that you feel that you are stepping into the essence of that archetype. Everyone is doing the same exercise so feel free to let loose and enjoy. Do not worry about anyone else's gesture; yours is perfect as it is. There really is no wrong way to do this. When you have each found your gesture or movement please come back to the circle.

After they had some time and guidance to find their gesture, we made a circle and one at a time we each shared the gesture and name of our archetype. It was an electrifying moment. The young people, the majority of whom were not performers, opened up and stood taller. The ones who I could barely hear just moments before took space with authority and full voice. The archetype gave them permission to bring outward an aspect of themselves they desired to express. Afterwards, they were given pen and paper to write their stream of consciousness in the voice of that archetype. Many shared their writing and expressed the realization that, if they chose, they could align themselves with the aspects of their hero and be like them. It was an empowering moment for us all.

One young man was particularly strong in his presentation. He had been in the United States only two years and was an honors student working to get in to college to be an architect. When it was his turn, he stepped forward, waved his arm backwards then forwards, grounding to the earth with full force and exclaimed, "Liberator!" I could feel in that single gesture not only the power of that archetype, but also the story this young man carried in his body of being on his own treacherous hero's journey. I imagined what it must have been for him crossing the desert on his own to make a better life for himself. He saw himself, or his hero at that moment, as a liberator. This movement resonated for many in the circle. By choosing this archetype, he was liberating himself and by extension others. He had great purpose in his voice and pride in his body. It is one of the most satisfying moments of my teaching career, to have guided that physically conscious embodiment of who that young man is striving to be. I hope he carries that archetype and leans on it when he needs to.

Five Archetypes for the Great Actor

The Fool, The Lover, The Shape Shifter, The Storyteller, and The Trickster

The five central great actor archetypes are The Fool, The Lover, The Shape Shifter, The Storyteller, and of course, The Trickster. All great actors are accessing each of these archetypes through the roles they play. Next are some descriptions of these archetypes and their value to us as actors.

The Fool

What would we be without this archetype? Well, for one thing, really boring. The Fool is the humbler in the room. Anyone is fair game for his jokes. The Fool is disruptive, disrespectful, blasphemous, rude, lewd, and speaks the truth like no other. Any actor worth their salt has some Fool within them and pays tribute to this powerful archetype. Being in The Fool archetype is not comfortable; it can be terribly embarrassing and painful. But we inhabit that space in order for others to see how wonderfully ridiculous humanity is.

KENT
This is not altogether fool, my lord.

FOOL.
No, faith, lords and great men will not let me; if I had a monopoly out, they would have part on't. And ladies too, they will not let me have all the fool to myself, they'll be snatching.

—William Shakespeare, *King Lear*

The Fool has the amazing ability to show culture's absurdities, to throw the veil off pretension, and uncover hidden truths. Great Fools like Buster Keaton, Mabel Normand, Peter Sellars, Carol Burnett, Eddie Murphy, Maya Rudolph, Steve Colbert, Mindy Kaling, and Amy Poehler have the ability to make us adore them while ridiculing us at the same time. They can be extremely powerful in revealing our culture's darkness in a way that can be palatable to an audience. *Dr. Strangelove* turns out to be a more effective film on the issue of the atomic bomb than *Fail Safe*. The former uses comedy to speak about the dangers of nuclear weapons; the later, drama. In this case, the comedic approach wins.

The Fool plays that role in order to get you to laugh, let your guard down, and then slips the dagger of truth. You know that moment when you are asked to do something in class or rehearsal that feels embarrassing? You know that feeling when your heart drops because you realize you are on the spot to do some clownish thing that frightens you? You have been chosen to do an improv of your scene, or pretend you are a gorilla, or invent a song about being a hairdresser in Transylvania? Do yourself a favor and call on Fool to step in and claim the space, leading you to glory. Giving in to Fool is tremendously rewarding because Fool will take whatever is handed to them, to the very outer limits, and relishes it. Fool never apologizes, but brandishes their wit and skill with great bravado. What is painful is not giving into Fool or to give in only part way. There is nothing half-assed about Fool energy. It is just about the bravest archetype on the planet.

If you do not give into Fool, you will be left out there hanging. But if you submit to Fool, oh boy, you will find yourself doing the most amazing things you never knew you were capable of. You will fly, you will soar, you will be the noble Fool.

Fool has nothing to prove. Fool has seen EVERYTHING and that wisdom leads to becoming a Fool. Without jokes, Fool's heart would crack wide open and the sorrow pouring forth would drown the earth. Fool is fully present and a great listener. They watch everything and allow themselves to be the perfect mirror for their audience. Fool bravely releases humor through the most painful of insights. Fool says, "It's not so serious! Look how silly I am! Shouldn't I get off my high horse?" Fool is a lifesaver.

Take a moment to think about and feel your relationship with Fool. Is Fool someone you intensely avoid or welcome? Are you uncomfortable in Fool's presence? Chances are that if you run away from Fool you are resisting an essential component of being an actor. Give in to Fool and you will see that you will make leaps in your work. Conversely if you rely too much on Fool you may find yourself as the actor audiences can only see in The Fool role. This may be what you want and there are many wonderful actors who devote their careers to being Fool exclusively. But if you want to play dramatic roles as well, if you want to have range, you will need to give Fool their due and develop other archetypes as well for balance.

The Lover

Oh dear Lover, what a mess you have often gotten us actors into! We fall in love so easily and we forget sometimes that it is through you we were carried away while playing that role, leaving us to pick up the pieces when the show or shoot is over. This archetype gets us into deep trouble, but without them we are lost as performers. As with the Falling in Love with the Room Exercise, The Lover archetype has an open heart and leads us to not only loving our stage and screen partners, but also loving the worlds we create, the words written for us, the choreography placed on our bodies, the objects we touch, the designers who let us plunge into lush worlds, etc. The Lover leads us to sensuality and without sensuality there is no actor. I want to be clear; this does not mean sexuality necessarily. Sensuality is something all great actors access. I like to use the example of great actor and filmmaker Charles Laughton who seems to have been born an old funny looking man. He became famous playing *The Hunchback of Notre Dame*. As unattractive as many thought he was, he was an amazingly sensual actor. It was that sensuality that drew us to him and brought us to tears with his touching portrayals. His film *Night of the Hunter* is considered a classic and taught in film schools all over the world. It is by working through our senses and with our sensuality that we as performers come alive.

Great actors know what they love. They also must know what their characters love and what they are willing to die for. The Lover helps us get to the stakes of our work, to make it urgent and necessary. There is nothing tepid in Lover; they are on fire with the passion they are obsessed with. That passion is essential for our work to have meaning. I love the New York-based American ensemble company UNIVERSES, founded by Artistic Directors Mildred Ruiz-Sapp and Steven Sapp. I have seen them perform since their early days from the South Bronx doing electrifying spoken word theater at PS122 in New York City. The moment they stepped on stage you felt glad to be alive; that is how passionate and charismatic they are as performers. Thirty some odd years later, that still rings true. The ensemble once said that it is no use getting out there on the stage if you're not "going to throw it down." An easy performance is not an option for them. The Lover archetype makes sure you are holding that passion to always "throw it down."

The Shape Shifter

Shape Shifter, you are a marvel. You are so grounded in your process that you are able to transcend and make great leaps out of who you are and what you know. You do this convincingly, with authority, and with total believability. You are so masterful at this that you have at times made your own family members and dearest loved ones say, "I didn't know it was you up there!" There is a legend that Marlon Brando could convince people from other countries that he was speaking their language. They fell for it because of his authority. They blamed themselves for not being able to hear well, which is why they did not understand what he was saying!

Shape Shifter, you connect deeply and transmigrate to the character you are working on. You transmute. You slither out of your skin and envelop yourself in that empathic place that allows you to see through another's eyes, hear what they hear, see what they see, and feel what they feel. You are sometimes uncomfortable in your own skin and you leap into other bodies to seek refuge from yourself. You are the actor people call versatile and you relish those unique abilities. You are a transformer, without the special effects. People who see what you do say your performances are nothing short of miraculous.

This archetype is thrilling to witness for an audience. I have seen actors with nothing but their skill and imagination change the planes of their faces, their gaze, the quality of movement, even their way of being. It is one thing to have the top Hollywood makeup artists superficially creating that transformation, and entirely another when that transformation comes from within.

Tom Hardy of *Peaky Blinders*, *The Revenant*, and *Warrior*, among many other fine works, is one of the great shape-shifting actors of all time. His transformations go far beyond great costumes, makeup, and dialect work. You can see a deep internal shift take place and he reveals characters that seem to be brought forth from his bones. He is an actor who deeply listens to where his body and imagination lead him in his process. He channels and calls forth these characters from an ancient source. It is mesmerizing work. I encourage shape shifting to happen not just from the externals. Later on in the chapter on character building exercises, we will touch on some tools that we can use to mine that kind of depth required for real shape shifting.

The Storyteller

The Storyteller has something passionate to share and holds the attention of an audience. If we cannot hold their attention, we are lost. A good actor must be a good storyteller, knowing when to begin the tale, when to hold off a bit for suspense, when to lean in when needed, and when to give it all they got at the right moment.

We must be that entity that transverses different spaces. To do this we must operate from the medial within. Clarissa Pinkola-Estes describes the medial as "that wild and knowing part of the psyche that can also traverse the world of the soul and the world of humans." It is a place of contradiction, as all artistic endeavors possess. We are both ourselves as well as the character. We mean what we say and we don't. We are having the character's experience and we are not. Liminal space is where the artist lives, where The Storyteller dwells within us. It is enchanted, powerful ground from which the imagination emerges. The imagination is called forth and happily comes running when we accept and submit to this medial plane.

I love watching where musicians go when they play. They are so clearly in a world between worlds. They are accessing territory that is neither fully awake nor asleep. The artistic act is the bridge between all these worlds, and the soul yearns for that space. When in that space, we are reminded of where we come from. The creative act is a resoundingly spiritual communion. This medial plane is The Storyteller's terrain. The Storyteller has all ground covered and traverses these different spaces with ease—one foot in the heavens, the other on earth. The Storyteller speaks to and with the dead, as well as its audience. They are the ones who transport their audiences by their mere presence. There is nothing eager about The Storyteller; they wait for the audience to come to them.

The Storyteller is also a Healer. I conducted an acting workshop for the theater group Teatro Jornalero (Day Laborers Theater) in the Malibu Canyon Forest. Here is what I remember:

To the left of me is a man in his 60s with grey hair at his temples. His worn and deeply creviced hands reveal a lifetime of hard work. He moves his swollen fingers in the air and pivots them with tremendous grace. This gentle movement at first seems improbable coming from this stocky older man, but soon becomes transcendent. He is at home with the gesture; the gesture is at home with him. His hands turn in as he presses them to his heart, tears stream down his cheeks, the sun brightening his forehead.

This was part of a culminating exercise. They had recently formed a company out of members of a recent Cornerstone Theater production. This was the company's retreat in order to make plans for the future, take workshops with local theater artists, enjoy their time in the forest together, and expand their training. This actor/day laborer had been asked to share a physical gesture with the other participants standing in a circle beside him. The gesture was to convey, without words, what the actor was taking with them from the workshop. We had been doing theater games, Contact Improvs, and other exercises for a few hours. Many people were making specific sensory connections, remembering home. Project ideas were surfacing and emotions were stirring.

The man looks at me. It is his turn. Everyone in the circle is aware of the authentic place from which the man is building his gesture. He had just done an exercise by a tree that brought him to a particular spot he had played in as a child in his hometown in Mexico. He is open and vulnerable. In the circle he begins to move, bringing all of himself to it. His large belly becomes supple and twists. He fearlessly moves his large waist and thick body in ways that are balletic. Everyone feels the power, grace, and truth of his gesture. Everyone is moved and enchanted by his sharing, his story of appreciation.

This is an experience that I often recall with great appreciation. It was a seminal moment for me. This man's particular contribution became one of my most memorable events as an artist. Here I felt the full impact of The Storyteller as Healer archetype. I could see in that moment of expression how this actor had been taken to a new place, a place of healing through the work. By extension, he had healed those of us around him. The memory of that moment at the tree earlier had carried him to a specific sensory memory that opened up his heart. Afterwards he shared with me how important it had been to allow himself to be graceful and to share with others a part of him he never felt he could reveal. Here was a man who made his living by his physical strength for decades. In his home he had to show strength as the primary breadwinner and the person responsible for getting his family through the enormous pressures of living in a country that was aggressively trying to deport them. But through the exercise he could let go of those masks he wore and free himself on a soul level as an artist. His storytelling was with his body and had great power for us all who witnessed it.

The Trickster

I leave Trickster for last because of their centrality and importance. The Trickster has a little bit of the demon in them; they are the outlaw. That somewhat devilish and non-benevolent nature is also a part of the Duende that Lorca wrote about. It is a combination of light and dark. That "trickiness" in The Trickster is incredibly energizing for the performer. It gives us our power and mystery. The Trickster also reminds us that in every story there is a lesson, oftentimes a bittersweet one. The Trickster is the carrier of that lesson.

Trickster is beyond The Fool and surpasses her in creatively sabotaging herself as an example to others. Trickster practices the holy craft of deception tied to the cosmic scope of painful truths. It is the bravest of archetypes, destined to wander alone while the ancestors whisper the teachings they must carry. Unwillingly, Trickster brings forward those lessons while finding a way to jab the ancestors along the way. No one is immune from her cutting wisdom, not even Trickster herself.

Trickster lives between worlds. There is a great story that appears in different versions around the world, the story of the Neutral Angels. In the war between God and Satan, the Neutral Angels took no sides and offered a stone of peace. They brought this stone from Heaven and as it came to Earth, the stone was scorched black. It is the Black Stone of Islam, or The Holy Grail, depending on the source for the story. It is an ancient stone set on the eastern corner of a mosque in Mecca. These Neutral Angels are very much like artists. We need to place ourselves in between: in between perspectives, in between being awake and asleep, in between being part of the culture, while also remaining outcasts. No great storyteller, actor, or artist was fully in one world. Remember the great Tom Stoppard quote, "We're actors, we're the opposite of people." While others choose and need to forget, the artist's job is to remember. We walk in between the living and dead, the real and imagined, and the rich fertile ground of our creativity.

4

NOIR

The Emergence of a Genre

Film Noir is a genre of film that was coined by the French, thus the French name, for black and white films of the late 1930s to early 1950s that shared a certain urban nihilistic aesthetic. There are countless books on the subject and many ideas on what truly coins a Noir film. Most Noir experts cite *The Maltese Falcon* as the first Noir, with *A Touch of Evil* ending the original cycle of the genre. Many contemporary TV shows and films reference, emulate, or make homage to the genre. The film *Devil in a Blue Dress* starring Denzel Washington is a contemporary Noir, as are the television series *Boardwalk Empire* and *Narcos: Mexico*. The actors are channeling great Noir performances.

Noir films are connected to the emergence of the urban city in the American landscape. The films often have a loner male lead who is the embodiment of a tough, urban American male figure and the dangerous, seductive woman. These characters emerged from an anxiety in the American psyche of the shifting world and the rise of industrialism. The people making Noirs did not know they were doing just that. The French saw these certain themes coming out of the hard-boiled American films and coined the term. Noir is a genre referenced and repeated time and time again; it is always being reconnected to and reimagined. It has great energy as a style of work. It has ties to German Expressionism and the prevalent doom related to World War II where humanity had reached a level of being able to destroy everything living on the planet. In the Noir film *Kiss Me Deadly* the earth is destroyed all together by an atomic bomb. It is a tough-as-nails genre where no one is sweet and the good cop is a rarity, a big change from previous films or even other films of the same era.

Jazz greatly influenced the crime novelists who gave birth to Noir. Without jazz, we might not have those great rhythmical pieces of glorious text like this one from director Howard Hawks' *The Big Sleep*:

> *I didn't ask to see you. I don't mind if you don't like my manners, I don't like them myself. They are pretty bad. I grieve over them on long winter evenings. And I don't mind your ritzing me, or drinking your lunch out of a bottle, but don't waste your time trying to cross-examine me.*
>
> —Phillip Marlowe

Humphrey Bogart delivers this text in the film on one breath with the exhilaration of a great saxophone solo. Similar to Shakespeare, Noir texts require us to sustain long thoughts on one breath and to keep the energy through to the end of the line. This is no small task, so it is a terrific and fun challenge for actors to sink their teeth into this rich vibrant text.

The Power of Stillness

The Noir work I have done for over 20 years has helped my students make invaluable discoveries. Noir is the module where they step into their unapologetic power as performers. They find the power of stillness and grace, as well as the ability to convey their story with economy and ease. I begin this section of training in the first weeks of our work together, asking my students to watch ahead of time a few classic Film Noirs such as *Double*

Indemnity, The Maltese Falcon, Laura, and *The Big Sleep.* I also assign them to read Raymond Chandler's exquisite short story, *Red Wind.* There are many reasons to start with Noir. I consider this material to help with "actor plies" and some very basic, necessary actor techniques. Central to this work is developing the power of stillness. As a performer you need to be acutely aware, as opposed to self-conscious, of your surroundings and the messages your body language is sending. If you are moving around too much or fidgeting, whether out of nerves or physical habits, you will be taking the focus away from what you are doing and saying. The foundation for good acting is having the power of stillness through ease. In Noir there is no room for shuffling your legs around, or playing with your hair, or emphasizing text with your head and face, or moving your arms around to show dramatic intensity. Noir performance should communicate a very focused, relaxed, and powerfully sensual body.

I have heard people say that presence is something you are born with, and to a certain extent I believe that is true; yet, I have also seen actors develop the power of presence through the Noir work. Through stillness with ease, your eyes come alive and inner thoughts become crystal clear. That clarity of thought is another actor essential.

Detective and Femme Fatale

Another reason for Noir is to work on two important archetypes, the *Femme Fatale* and the *Detective.* Both the Femme Fatale and the Detective are important for the actor to engage with. An actor must have the yin and the yang; the archetypal masculine as well as archetypal feminine. Versatility and depth emerges from these parts of us through our work. When actors fully give in and make this leap, they find all kinds of hidden resources for them to bring into characters of their own. The women often find more resonance in their voices, the men more grace in their movements, and the transgender and non-binary actors release into performing archetypes they are not usually given the opportunity to explore. Most of my students often feel that the material gives them permission to explore the archetypal gender that they are drawn to initially. For some this may be more challenging than others, but all end up finding more range and specific areas they need to continue to develop.

All actors are detectives of human behavior. We watch people. It tends to be one of our favorite things. Through watching others we find our characters. We must embrace this part of our craft and acknowledge that we are detectives. When we pick up a text, we are looking for the clues the writer has given us. Once we inhabit that Detective archetype, we carry that thirst for investigation in our work for the rest of our lives. We love the danger of our process; how exciting it is to be close to "solving" a scene or finding the walk of a character. Embodying this archetype gets us to the essentials of the work; that nose to the ground, can't sleep until I solve it, exhilarating place in the process.

The other side of the classic Noir archetype is the Femme Fatale. Much has been written about whether this archetype, as a male fantasy, is a victim. I see her differently. I see her as a groundbreaking character for her time. The Femme Fatale in Noir films was a force of nature, one that decided her destiny. Yes, her destiny was almost always tragic, but so are all the characters in Noir. It is a fatalistic genre forged out of the horrific events around WWII and the atomic bomb. It is a genre that comes to being because, for the first time in human history, human beings can destroy the entire planet. The Femme Fatale knows who she is, what she wants, and risks everything for it. She also contains another archetypal essential for actors: the Seducer. When we cultivate the Femme Fatale, we are playing with some Trickster energy and allowing the graceful and sensual to fill our bodies and voices. All actors are Seducers. In order to hold the stage or camera, something in us says, "Watch me!" The best actors hold our attention and seduce us into doing just that. We are awake and alive through our sensorial experiences. A good actor is keenly primed to embody in a moment the richest of sensory memories. To be sensorily attuned means to submit to the land of the sensual.

So the Femme Fatale is the Seducer in us; she is deliciously sensual and loves being in her skin. Everything she touches gets infused with grace and lusciousness. Holding a cigarette becomes ferociously erotic! The key here is to find that fiery subtlety that the great Femme Fatales in Noir, such as Lauren Bacall, Barbra Stanwyck, and Jane Greer, do breathtakingly well. I mean just look at those Queens of Noir move and talk! They couldn't care less what you think of them. They hold their own. Here are some extraordinary performers and contemporary Femmes Fatales in media who unapologetically inhabit their version of this powerful archetype: Jurnee Smolett and Jamie Chung of Lovecraft Country, Fernanda Urrejola of Narcos Mexico, Helen McCrory of Peaky Blinders, Billy Porter of Pose, Julia Garner of Ozark, Thandy Newton of Westworld, Anya Taylor Joy of The Queen's Gambit, and Kelly Reilly of Yellowstone. If you want to learn from masters, watch those performers channel that fierce Femme Fatale energy.

Through the Detective archetype we have the part of us who digs into the material; the Femme Fatale offers us sensuality. We need both as we discover our work to take us to great lengths as performers. They are the bedrock of our acting practice and keeping them close will open worlds for us. I have my students, regardless of their gender, work on both archetypes. In the exercise to come you will see how there is room for whatever gender preference to reap rewards from this material. I leave it to my students ultimately to choose what archetype to primarily focus on, but encourage them to weave back and forth between the two. I encourage the dancing between the archetypes even in performance. This is an expansive exercise, not meant to diminish or play into stereotypical gender roles. These are archetypes of masculine and feminine characters, but that does not mean they are necessarily male and female.

The idea is to find YOUR power in these archetypes, not to imitate anyone else. What is your version of the Femme Fatale or the Detective? They both have a great deal to offer if you wish to explore. You do not have to sound like Lauren Bacall or Humphrey Bogart, but you are asked to find your power through stillness, your sensuality, and your economy through ease.

Noir Café Improv

I assign my students to choose sections of Noir text from the films noted before and Chandler's Red Wind. I also ask them to come in with five gestures for the Femme Fatale and five for the Detective. They are assigned to dress however they wish in exploring these two archetypes, but keeping in mind to be as close to the period as they can. It is important to bring in clothes that help them feel different and move them away from comfort. Some actors choose one of the archetypes to fully dive into costume wise; others choose to play with elements of costume for both archetypes.

I provide fedoras for those who want to play with that element. I place clip lights around the room to give a mysterious feel to the space. I play instrumental jazz music such as Dexter Gordon and John Coltrane. Once they are dressed and the ambiance is set, we begin.

Find a space in the room to stand and get centered. Listen to the music. Let it affect you and fill your body. Now slowly begin to move into the gestures you brought to work on. Move into each gesture as slowly as you can. The intent is not to get to a position, but to experience the feelings that arise as you move towards that gesture. If your movements jerk suddenly or you find yourself rushing, take a moment to invite yourself to slow down and breathe. Let yourself be like water as you move in and out of your gesture. Take all the time you need. Be in your own time. Luxuriate in your movements, in the feeling of being in your body. Allow sensuality in your body to come forward. Keep supple and loose. Even for those tough Detective gestures, find fluidity and ease. Breathe.

Take this process for each gesture you brought in: five for Femme Fatale and five for the Detective. Do not worry while exploring your Detective gestures if you are dressed head to toe as the Femme Fatale; see how they feel and emerge in your Femme Fatale dress. Let this masculine energy come through in those gestures regardless.

Once you have fully explored the gestures, in a voiced whisper play with some of the text you brought in. Do not worry about it "fitting" the text with the gesture. Be unapologetic in this exploration. This is about finding your power, your version of these archetypes. No one else has to look or sound like you. If your voice sounds jarring to you, take it again. Look for that economy and ease. Use your awareness work to simply and non-judgmentally take note of what you are observing while doing this. Be patient and kind to yourself. Nice and easy.

Now expand your awareness to the others in the room. Take them in. Notice who of these characters you are drawn to, who repelled by. Keep in mind that everyone in the room is dangerous, and you have a secret. Begin to walk around the space. Continue to hear the music. Allow yourself to engage with others in the room. You are in Café Noir. Try out some of your gestures and text with those you come in contact with. Take it slow, no rush. Within this slow world, begin to explore on occasion some quick dynamic moves or pieces of text. Keep in mind:

Everyone in here is dangerous.
You have a secret.
Someone here has information you need and must get.

After a few minutes of this, you can find your own relationships and language in the improv. Weave in and out of the text you brought in and begin to explore your own Noir language. This part of the improv should take at least 20 minutes, so the world has a chance to evolve and relationships thicken.

When leading this exercise I watch over to make sure everyone is safe in the room. It is always a joy to observe how the room becomes electric, charged with the energy of the genre. As tough as the exercise is for some, everyone gets to a place where they spiral into themselves and find more comfort in these archetypes. For many it gives them permission to step into an adulthood they had not felt empowered to take on before. This is especially true of the undergrads I work with. I have had many actors confront their puritanical upbringings that made the sensuality part of this exercise very painful. In time, most are able to move towards enjoying their bodies in ways they never felt they had a right to. This is sometimes the hardest part of this work, helping people breathe through defenses and traumas that close them up as performers.

I usually finish the improv by whispering to everyone in the group "someone here has a gun" and to one of the students "you have the gun." The person with the gun ends up shooting one of the other people to get the thing they need. We never use real props, miming a finger in the air will do. For a room full of actors the commitment behind this can get very intense, and also very fun. At the end of the improv I give the students a few minutes to write down observations, awarenesses, and any favorite improv text that emerged. Plays have been drawn out of this exercise!

MARISSA: Ok so let me hear a bit about what you observed. What were you aware of through this exercise? And remember to use sensorily grounded language.

JULIANA: I felt very uncomfortable at first; my shoulders and jaw were really tight, especially when I was working by myself. I just was jumping out of my skin. Nothing felt right. But then I looked over at

Terry and he was being a jerk, commanding me to walk over to him, and it sparked something in me. I moved into my Femme Fatale gesture with more strength, I felt very grounded and that I had a lot of power over him. My chest felt fluttery and I noticed my legs stopped gripping. I just did my gesture and walked away from him and I could feel his eyes following me. It really felt great, like I was taller than anyone. And my voice really dropped in when I walked over to Shaina and spoke my text.

MARISSA: Yes, I saw you and Shaina have a very dynamic exchange, what was that?

SHAINA: Ok, so I saw Juliana walking away from Terry and I had decided she was the one I needed to get information from. And I thought the best way would be to befriend her.

JULIANA: (laughing) Yeah, I wasn't expecting you to shoot me later.

SHAINA: (laughing) Right, well, that was my secret you see. And I noticed how much more resonant and grounded your voice was when you talked to me. You really sounded different than when we were having lunch earlier. It almost made me sad that I had to kill you.

MARISSA: Do you see how these simple directives charged up the space? Having a secret is very empowering. The CalArts Alum and great actor/clown Bill Irwin told a great story when he came here a few years ago and met with the students. He said he always goes to an audition with two different socks on. That way he knows something the audition-ers don't. He's got a secret. Having that secret for a performer is very powerful. And Juliana, that grounding you felt in your body and voice, and that Shaina noticed, is something you want to return to.

TERRY: Well I definitely felt cut down when Juliana turned away, so I watched the women for a while and that's when Jorge came over to me. He said, "Have you got it?" I remembered that we need to affirm our partners' impulses so I immediately said, "Yes, but you won't get it until I get what I want."

MARISSA: Nice, there's a good example of the first rule of improv as taught to me by my mentor George Morrison—affirm your partner's impulses with "yes, and"! What you did Terry is raise the stakes, not just affirm the gift Jorge gave you by giving you the clue that you have something that Jorge wants. Excellent.

Something that has time and again been said in the feedback circle we do afterwards is that there is an elasticity of space that happens between partners, a charged energy. The actors begin to feel their power through accessing these unapologetic archetypes. It is as if they expand and get larger before our eyes. With the students who have worked together for some time, they are able to report back changes they saw in each other that they had never seen before. Some have terrible difficulties with the stillness at first, but when they hear from others how strong they become when they are still, their confidence grows and they give in to that more and more. The unnecessary movement is really just we as actors apologizing for our existence. It is nothing less than believing we are not enough and need to "do" something. This work reminds us that *we are more than enough and we do not have to do but just to be.* The main things we look to gain through this material are—

The Power of stillness
Sensuality through the archetypes
Unapologetically taking up space
Finding economy and ease with our bodies and text

5

THE BODY TEXT CONNECTION

Excavating Scenes and Monologues From a Mythic View

The great actor is both attuned to what is resonating within while also connected to the external forces around them. Our process is similar to athletes who are trampolining from external impulses and internal assessment to action, in a constant river-like dance. We need to be nimble and in a state of readiness that allows us to spring from our impulses to respond to those around us without hesitation. Acting teachers often use the phrase "Get out of your head" as a directive. It is a little like, "Don't think of pink elephants." What we need are tools to change our focus and place us in the impulse driven readiness to be *out of our heads* and into our *liberated state of being*. I purposely did not use the word "body" because of course our heads are already in our bodies. We cannot separate mind from body.

Next I offer several exercises that I use with my students that make space for that duality, readiness, and liberated state of being. These exercises are pathways towards embodied performances where every cell in the actor's instrument is engaged, not just neck-up acting. The body/text connection is very important for the mythic approach. Contemporary neuroscientist Antonio Damasio, who wrote the book *Descartes Error*, speaks on the importance of feeling as intelligence. In fact, as infants our brain cells increase and get fired up when we are touched. Our feelings are our body's way of guiding us to make smart decisions. This connection between feeling, body, and brain is what is often left out in our processes in the West. We sit and do table work before anything else and perhaps leave behind the feelings that may not make logical sense as we work on our roles, but may hold great gifts for us. Rather than starting your process with table work, what happens if you move back and forth between the page and the body to find the revelations you need? I encourage you to use the following exercises amidst the rehearsal process to ensure you are not glued to your seat. We can easily get trapped in a linear, literal mind if all the choices we make as actors come from sitting and discussing at a table. The following exercises are meant to make sure we are listening to the text, being diligent as storytellers, coming up with the essential clues left for us by the writer, and including the body/poetic imagination. This last part is lacking far too often in the contemporary actor's process. That is why Don Cheadle works with a Jungian analyst on his roles. We want to open the portals to the imagination and to the unexpected; we cannot do that if the linear mind is leading. We need both the rational and the body/spirit loosed from the rational in the mythic process.

Our first step needs to be to approach our characters with an open heart. This is easier said than done so let us invite Kuan Yin to serve as a guide. Kuan Yin is the Chinese goddess of compassion, kindness, and mercy. The name means, "*She who observes all sounds of suffering in the world.*" Often depicted in white, she holds in one hand a vase containing the water of life, a willow branch in the other. Kuan Yin is a merciful problem solver who has a thousand arms and eyes in order to best serve those who need her aid.

Let the audience judge the role we are playing; that is not our job. We need to fully place ourselves in the character's shoes and express their version of the story. You can always tell when an actor is judging the role. I call it acting in quotes. There is a clear separation between them and the story they are telling. If we can get rid of the quotes, we have a fighting chance of doing our job fully. That empathy, the portal opened by Kuan Yin, is central to our work.

These exercises are meant to liberate and ignite your imagination. If an exercise is stifling to you, then move on and try another. Come back to it at another time. This is part of the treasure chest I like to help build for the actor. Take these exercises as they reveal themselves useful to you; leave them for another time if not.

Embodied Femme Fatale and Detective Text Work

Here is where you can put that fedora on and dive into the "facts" of the material you are working with and that red lipstick for the intuitive part of our process. If this is language-based theater, you will find "clues" in the text. If it is visual or dance-theater, the "clues" will be in the movements given or central images being explored. Whichever is the case, you will need both Detective and Femme Fatale at your side.

In our work as actors, we must allow ourselves to do both the left-brain digging of the Detective, as well as the right-brain of the Femme Fatale. The Detective leads us to clues from the writer, traps, etc., whereas the Femme Fatale takes us to the sensual parts of our work. One cannot exist without the other. If we focus on only one, there is imbalance. As you do these exercises, imagine that you are dancing between the two, inviting both to create the bridges between you and your material. If at some point it becomes too Detective heavy, step back and allow that Femme Fatale to slide in. Dance with the words and let your senses take over.

In keeping with the spirit of this approach, begin with asking yourself what you are most curious about in this script and the character you are working on. What questions do you have? What is pulling at you? What do you want to explore? What pops out for you? There is no need to answer the questions. Let them be there, presenting themselves and see where your process leads with your curiosity at the forefront. Our journey is not to understand. Understanding is overrated. Our process is to explore. If we reach for all the answers too soon, we close ourselves off from deeper impulses.

When working with actors, it is fascinating to me to see their reaction after I ask the question, "What are you most curious about with this role and this material?" I see a little light spark behind their eyes and a slight smile. It is as if they are accessing something mischievous, perhaps that is their Trickster. We search within our material for what pulls us in and fills us with wonder. That wonder is everything. When we are wondering, we are engaging fully with the task. When we wonder, we step out of the pedestrian and embrace childlike curiosity. We do not know it all, yet we are twirling around something that caught our imaginations. Let that curiosity guide you.

Headline

Knowing the headline for your scene is an idea that emerged after I was asked to speak at George Morrison's *New Actors Workshop* to his graduating actors, along with legendary film and theater director Mike Nichols. We had been invited to share our thoughts about the acting profession. Needless to say, I was tremendously honored to be sharing space with Mr. Nichols. One of the elements Mr. Nichols shared was the importance of knowing what "the event of the scene" was for an actor. He spoke about how you need to read the scene and know what is of primary importance. You must know what the primary part of the storytelling is that the audience must take away with them after they have experienced that particular scene. In order for the story to move forward, what does the audience need to know? This is something I had spoken about to my students countless times before, but I realized after hearing him speak that having a headline would be the best way to convey the urgency of this knowledge for the actor.

Look at the scene or monologue that you are working on. There are often several events that happen, but there is one of primary importance for the storytelling. Take some time before you land on just the right one. If it is a scene, be sure to discuss this with your partner or partners. Remember this is not what the character wants; this is the single most urgent piece of information the audience needs to carry the story forward. Keep your headline short and concise. In *The Cherry Orchard*, towards the end of Act Three, Lopakhin comes in very drunk after being at the auction for the estate. Many things happen in that scene but a headline that can serve the actors working could be: "Lopakhin announces buying the Cherry Orchard." This is the most pressing piece of news in the entire act of the play. Knowing this is essential to our work. It is helpful for this exercise to imagine that you are a journalist writing about that scene or monologue. What would that headline be? Be sure to include details and an active verb; this will help connect you to that all important WHY for your character within the story. Here is a more active version of the earlier headline: "Former servant Lophakin celebrates buying cherry orchard; Ranyevskaya loses legacy."

We need to be clear about our headlines to be good storytellers and serve the play. If the vision for the play by the lead artists, such as the director, is something different then, of course, change the headline accordingly. Having this storyline clarity and knowing our role in conveying that headline is an important and helpful tool for actors.

Another important element to the headline is to connect with our place in the story. How does my character propel this story, what is their place in this headline? If I know that I am able to connect with my ensemble and make the storytelling clear, rather than each of us doing our own thing at cross-purposes. It is important that all actors are working towards the same headline.

Picture Exercise

I give thanks to Mirah Love who shared this exercise with me. I have developed it and have found ways to incorporate this with text that is shared next.

Choose several images for your scene or monologue. Pick one for the exercise. You can do it with other images after you have done it with one. The image should be something representational but not necessarily literal. In other words, if I am working on Act Four of The Cherry Orchard, I do not want to choose an image of a literal cherry orchard being chopped down. What is the metaphor for the scene? Can you find images that express that metaphor? What does the scene feel like as an image? Let yourself be drawn to an image. It does not have to make sense. Trust where your imagination leads you. This last part is extremely important. You may not know now why you were drawn to a certain image, but you may understand later. Remember we are stirring the unconscious impulse; that is where our gold is. There is a reason why great writers, scientists, thinkers, etc. have their best ideas in the shower or on a walk. Our deepest answers emerge when we allow our minds and spirits to roam and interact with nature. Trust that.

Be sure that you have a hard copy of your image, do not use a phone or computer screen. It can be an image from an art book, post card, a photograph, etc.

Picture Exercise Done Alone

Place the image on the ground in front of you. Have your journal and something to write with nearby but not in the way. Make sure you have a clear space in front of you to move around freely. If you can, set up a smart phone or video recording device to capture the exercise. Have a timer ready for three minutes to be set after you are centered.

Close your eyes. Take three easy, full, luxurious breaths. Begin with the Centering Exercise from Chapter 1. Bring the feeling of the scene to your body and breath. Be sure to allow your body to be aligned and your breath to be free, flowing in and out of your body. Allow whatever comes up for you to be present; do not run away. Now open your eyes. Set the timer to start and look again at the image.

During those three minutes look at the image on the ground and let it inspire your movement. Let it be non-stop, as with stream of conscious writing. This is stream of consciousness moving. Slow down when you need to. Allow for a diversity of physical expression. Break patterns and explore. No need to make it a dance but feel free if you want to. You are simply allowing yourself to move freely using the image as an inspiration.

Afterwards, jot down in your journal three to five movements you enjoyed or that felt good when you were doing the exercise. Be sure to revisit the moves you are choosing through your body before notating them in your journal. You can reference the video if you like.

Picture Exercise With Three

In this version it is ideal to work with people you are doing the scene with, or who are working on the same script/project as you. This exercise works well for both on camera or on stage performance, as well as dance-theater. Each actor has an image to work with and will be moving to the image they have chosen. One actor is the Mover, one is the Narrator, and the other is the Observer. You will switch after every two minutes so everyone has an opportunity to be all three. The Narrator looks at the image and offers the Mover words to inspire them that are directly coming to them from the image they are seeing. It can be combinations of actual colors in the image, the shapes, etc., but also feelings that may arise. The Narrator is riffing off the image, much like a jazz improvisation. The Mover moves freely in response to the words they are offered by the Narrator. The key here is to allow for the body to be taken and to flow from one move to the next. The body imagination must be liberated. What is most important is that the Narrator continuously offers words and phrases for the Mover, who continually moves. The Observer watches from the side, standing and mirroring moves they see the Mover do that strike them or that they are drawn to. After the two minutes both the Observer and the Mover jot down moves in the same way as earlier when the Mover worked alone.

You are always moving to the image you brought in but after a round of that you can switch and move to an image your partner brought in. When you have completed the cycle of three moves, you will have six to ten moves created through the exercise: three to five of your own and three to five from having observed.

Incorporating Picture Exercise With Text

Take your moves, whether from doing the exercise alone or with a group, and create a sequence. Allow one move to flow into the other or dynamically shift from one to the next. Make sure you have variety physically and are using your whole body. Let loose and free.

Now add text to your sequence. Allow yourself to be affected by the movement as you say the text. Let parts be slow and others quick and sharp. Shifting in vocal and physical variety is important.

This is a great way of "getting out of one's head" and finding physicality for your scene or monologue. By incorporating another person's moves you are getting out of your habitual patterns physically. It is a liberating exercise that connects your body, breath, imagination, and voice to work together on your scene or monologue. It can be used as an exploration or actual staging, depending on the style of work you are doing.

Stream of Consciousness Writing

This is a simple exercise that can lead to some wonderful surprises. Have your journal and something to write with next to you. Have a timer ready to be set for three minutes. Use one of the Centering Exercises. Bring to your body, mind, and spirit the scene or monologue you are working on. Imagine what your character is doing just before the scene starts. Really allow yourself to picture the story just before your entrance. Think of as many details as you can: Who is there, where are they, what are they doing, what are the sounds, smells, feelings? Open your eyes and start the timer. Now put pen to page and write without stopping in the voice of your character. Let them speak to you. Let the pen go. If you repeat words or say nonsense that is fine. Keep writing and imagining the thoughts that are swimming around in their head just before the scene or monologue.

Point of Entry

From the moment an actor is seen on stage they are telling a story. Before they have spoken a word their bodies are carrying their circumstances, state, place, and time. I call this the *Point of Entry*, or POE. Actors often rush into scenes and the audience has to do a great deal of catching up to find out who they are and what is going on. With a clear POE, you are letting the audience in and guiding them through your body and clarity of thought to what is driving you.

For this exercise focus on the moment that begins your monologue or scene. Extend it several minutes and present in class that extended moment, before text is spoken. Include in this silent exercise as many details as you can. When you present your work see if the classmates can guess at least some of the five basic actor questions (*Who am I?, Where am I?,*

What do I want?, *How do I get it?*, and *What is my obstacle?*). It is very important to embody in this exercise, rather than indicate. Perhaps the other actors only pick up on a few details such as: You are outside, you seem tired, you look like you've lost something, etc.

> It is 1988 and I am seeing Richard Foreman's Symphony of Rats at the Wooster Group's Performance Garage in New York City. I had not read anything about the play and was excited to see the latest work from this company that was quickly becoming my favorite. The house lights were still up as company member Ron Vawter stood to the side of the house with a light on him, waiting to make his entrance. We are in that place where the audience is still settling but the show has not seemingly begun. People begin to notice him but some of the audience is still fidgeting about and talking. I watch Mr. Vawter as he nervously stands off to the side, pulls a white cloth handkerchief from his pocket and dabs his forehead in shaky dabs, conveying someone in great anxiety. As I watched him, a thought ran through my mind, "He must be the president." Mr. Vawter moved onto the stage and the audience quieted. We soon learned that he was playing the president of the United States. How did he do that? How were his thoughts so clear that he conveyed, before uttering a word, that he was so specifically the president of the United States? This is an example I use with all my students. I realized then that our thoughts are tangible. If I am thinking of that ham sandwich backstage, the audience will feel my restlessness and unfocused energy. The magic of what we do is to fully inhabit our stories through our bodies and state of being that the audience understands our thoughts, our state, and what we are experiencing.

Text-Based Scene and Monologue Work

Read the whole play of your scene or monologue. Now read it again. Perhaps you have done the stream of consciousness exercises described earlier; if not, please refer to that and do it for the play. Note the images, phrases, and words that came up. Now do the same for your particular scene or monologue. Have your image board in front of you and the moves you found in Picture Exercise ready. While working on the next sequence of exercises be sure to get up and refer to the image board, move into your gestures from the Picture Exercise, and let this be a dance between them all. Be careful not to just sit as you work with text-based material. The body needs to stay engaged and the imagination must be open and ready.

What Are the Facts?

Write down all the facts you have for your scene or monologue. List everything, including the location, stage directions, descriptions of characters, etc. These are the clues the writer has left for you to follow.

What Questions Do I Have?

Now that you have the essential facts, write out your questions about those facts. Go on, the Detective will come through when invited. When you have written the questions, consider them.

Let the questions be there on the page. No need to rush to easy answers. When do investigators go with their first or surface impulses? Most cases are not solved that way. There is one major difference between detectives and actors; while detectives ultimately want a solution, we as actors want to continuously engage with the facts and the questions of the material we are working on. Our work should never be "solved." There is no end to what a character has to offer us as it relates to discovering the role. The better the material, the more this is true.

There may be questions that you have in regards to time period or culture. It is very important to write all these questions down. Never assume. It is your job to investigate and leave no stone unturned. The same is true if you find yourself unsure of the meaning of a word. Look it up. Be a thorough investigator. Do not let laziness rule. Playwrights are constantly leaving us "clues" to contemplate and make sense of by the end of the play. You need to practice picking up those clues and following their lead. Be sure to have strong footing on the five basic actor questions:

Who am I?
Where am I?
What do I want?
How do I get it?
What is my obstacle?

So, you have listed the facts and questions. Now write down all that is said about your character in the play and all that others say about them. Look at both lists. How does that inform you? Are there differences between the facts your character thinks of themself and what others think of them? What does that mean to you? How are you similar to your character? How are you different? What do you share? What points of connection do you have?

What Are the Traps?

All character portrayals have their "traps," which are those easy answers that make for a one- dimensional portrait. For example, one trap in playing the title character in Luis Alfaro's *Electricidad* based on Elektra, is that she is always enraged. There is no question Electricidad is furious with her mother, the murder of her father, and death of her brother, but she is filled with much more than anger. If there is no love for the mother she kills, there are no stakes or dramatic tension. We serve our process to go beyond the obvious and to be aware of the traps within the role. We need to delve deeply into the character's wants, needs, history, motives, obstacles, and soul's desires. If you are judging your character through your portrayal, you are doing that character and the material a disservice.

Archetypes to Find Colors and Range

As discussed in Chapter 3, working with both the light and shadow aspects of the archetype helps us move away from monotone portrayals and invites our imaginations in to the process. You can purchase archetype cards or look up on the Internet and you will discover there are hundreds. Be sure to work with an archetype rather than a stereotype. As soon as what you are working with has a race, ethnicity, gender, etc., it leaves the realm of archetype. As a reminder, archetypes can be of any race, gender, ethnicity, age, etc.

Use one of the Centering Exercises we have discussed and invite that archetype in. As you connect to the archetype, notice the feeling that comes along with this archetype and follow that. Now focus on the light aspect first. Step into that body. Find a gesture that goes with that archetype. Allow sound to follow that gesture. Let this be a full physical and vocal exploration. You can pull back later but for now release and express as freely and openly as you can while connecting to the light aspect. If you are not finding freedom and connection try another gesture and sound until you do. Take one line from your monologue. It can be approximate if not yet off book. Say the line while doing the gesture.

Do the same series with the shadow. Pick a different line/thought than the one you just used for the light aspect. Allow this to be completely different in your body and voice, as big a contrast as you can make. Now go from light to shadow, or vice versa, one at a time. Once you have done this exploration, pull back and see if you can keep the contrast you found but move from shadow to light or light to shadow with your lines as if you had a camera close up. Focus on making these shifts subtle and behind the eyes. You can have a wide variety of gradation.

This is a wonderful resource for finding those hills and valleys within our performances that include those details and surprises audiences want to witness. The following is a conversation that happened after my actors engaged in the preceding exercise and I asked them for their observations:

SONIA: That exercise surprised me.

MARISSA: What was surprising?

SONIA: Well, I thought I knew what I wanted to do when you began leading the exercise. I wasn't really connected to the gesture part of it. But I found that as soon as I was invited to release a sound, it took me to a place in my voice I rarely use. I cannot even remember ever sounding like that before. It felt really right for the character.

HENRY: I had a similar experience when I put the text to the gesture. I connected with an emotion I would never have come to but for finding it through this archetype. I'm not sure it's right for the monologue but it really helped me get out of the idea I had for him.

MARLEA: I really struggled to connect to the shadow. I think it is a little scary for me to go there.

MARISSA: Absolutely listen to your body about that. Take your time with this. It may not happen for you in the first round of exploring. But give it a shot. You might also try a different archetype, one that may not bring up so much discomfort for you.

TOBIE: I have been struggling with being more expressive. I get notes about being monotone. Even though I think I'm connecting to emotions, it doesn't seem to read that way. I was working with light and shadow with three different archetypes, contrasting ones, and I felt that using all of these from one thought to the next helped me be more expressive. I mean, you tell me. (*The other students affirm Tobie was more expressive.*)

ALEJANDRA: I think this exercise is helping me find detail. There is so little written about my character, so few clues as to what motivates her. It is really up to me to bring that forward. This helps me find that in an imaginative way.

MARISSA: The archetypes you are playing with give you permission to explore new territory. It can expand you out of comfort zones and allow for idiosyncratic impulses that can give your character that unpredictability and depth you want to see in a performance. And what is leading is not an idea, at least not intellectually. You are allowing for the body's intelligence to help you find it. It leads us to a multi-faceted prism of expression.

The Need to Speak

The great Argentinian writer Jorge Luis Borges in his essays *On Writing* published at Harvard shared the idea that all language is a translation. It is the feeling that creates language. That essence of meaning is key in determining how we communicate. This is very important for an actor to be aware of and seek connection to when discovering a new character's language and way of speaking. We must speak from the *need to speak*, connecting first to the feeling that gives rise to the words and then sharing the words that tumble out of us out of *necessity*. If we fail to do this, we have neck up acting. It may sound lovely and be accomplished with technique, but it is meaningless. Without the connection to feeling, the audience will see that we are merely reciting.

When we find that need to speak, we are also connecting to that all-important *why* for our characters. It is our full investment to that *why* that makes audiences lean in and hang on our words. If you have that investment, the audience will want to listen and follow you. Our *why* is the heart of the assignment with the role we are playing.

Operative Words

Stand on one side of the room, your partner on the other. Say the operative words in your text as if they were bullets landing on your partner across the room. If you want, start off by sending your hand out into space with the word. Then work towards the words having that impact through stillness. Be sure not to yell. Let the voice be grounded when you do this. What is important is finding the emphasis without straining yourself. You will know when you strain because your voice will hurt. If that happens, stop, connect with your breath, and try again.

What New Terrain Are You Seeking?

With every role we take on, we expand as actors. One character may help us find new vocal resonance, emotional resources, or abilities to command an audience through a long story. Each role gives us an opportunity to expand as artists. I ask the performers I work with, what will working on this character open up for you? What gift does this role offer you? When we ask ourselves this question, we can begin to consciously use our material, whether chosen or assigned, as a map. It activates us to engage the part with agency, keeping our desires for growth front and center. I love seeing a student's eyes light up with the prospect that the role will get them to do something they have never done before. That passionate engagement is what will take their work to new depths.

6

SPOKEN IMPROVS

When working on improvisations that incorporate text, this four-step exercise uses the body as the pathway for the words, leading you into spoken improv with a partner. The sequence of the exercise moves from Mirror, Rebound, Space Rebound, and finally Scene. The approach originated with my mentor George Morrison. I then utilized these exercises with the Perceptor Theater, an improv group I co-founded along with film stars Stanley Tucci and Ving Rhames.

These exercises and approaches to improv, while seemingly traditional, are mythic in that they center on the body leading, rather than the rational mind. These improvs allow for tremendous flights of the imagination. Nothing is too extreme if the actor is completely and totally invested. What brings these exercises to the mythic is how you as an actor invest in them with your creativity and allow for the idiosyncratic. The audience will buy it, no matter how out there, if you are committed.

Mirror

This is a classic exercise done in all beginning acting classes. It is a great "plié" for actors of all levels and a wonderful way to connect with your partner.

Face your partner. Stand in a neutral position and look into each other's eyes. Begin by synchronizing your breath. Breathe together with ease. Freely flowing on the inhalation, then exhalation. Allow yourself to see the face in front of you as your face, the body (through your soft focus) as your body. In time you will begin to move. Resist the temptation to try to make it happen. Don't worry, it will. Dive into the presence of your partner, your "image." If someone were to come around to observe, they would not be able to tell who was leading and who was following. Explore this part of the exercise for at least six minutes. Make sure you are breathing together and allowing for full body exploration. Keep eye contact at all times. Stay together moving simultaneously and seamlessly.

This is the version that I learned from George and it has one important difference to most Mirror exercises. There is no leader and no follower. So how does movement happen? The actors are *taken* by something between them.

Rebound

Once you have been in Mirror for at least six minutes, begin to move into Rebound. The image of a seesaw is a good one to help imagine this exercise. One partner starts with a sound and physical gesture. The other partner then "responds" or "rebounds" to that with a sound and physical gesture of their own. The sound and movement should be both simple and rhythmic, so that once the partner rebounds you are quickly moving back and forth rhythmically. You want to continue repeating this exchange without escalating or changing it in any way. Stay in this initial sound and movement for at least six to ten exchanges with your partner. Then one of you changes it, introducing a new sound and physical gesture. The other partner responds with something new too. Exchange these six to ten times and change it up again. Continue to repeat. Use as much of your voice and body as you can. Free it up. Keep the channel open. Once you have done the Rebound exercise, return to the original position you started in.

Space Rebound

The next phase moves you into the soft focus, after having direct eye contact with your partner in Mirror and Rebound. Here you change your focus to the space in and around and between you and your partner. One person changes that space by moving a part of their body in slow motion and as though you are moving through a substance like molasses. Once you come to a complete stop, the partner responds moving their body to change the space between them. The main thing here is to use your bodies to listen to each other. It is not about getting to a certain pose or position or shape; the point is to feel the space as you change it. Remember that you are changing the space in and around and between you and your partner. Do this as slowly as you can. This is a very different dynamic than the often high-energy animated quality of Rebound.

Scene

This section requires an outside leader to start and end the improv. I use a whistle in class for this four-step exercise. It helps when the room gets raucous and becomes hard to hear a lone voice over the improvs. I ask the students to resist the temptation, which can be difficult, to plan their improv while in Space Rebound. I always can tell when someone is purposely moving into poses they think will be a good place to start an improv scene. The purpose of Space Rebound is to connect to your partner on a different level than the previous exercises and to be in your body. Thinking of a clever scene pulls us away from where our real gold is, being in the here and now. Encourage the actors to "give up the plan."

When they have done a nice exploration of Space Rebound for at least three minutes, I call "Scene!" Now the actors need to use their current position in some way to justify the start of a scene. I have made certain rules that I share beforehand for them to follow during their improvs:

The performers *cannot use their own names or be in the setting they are currently in.* At CalArts, I say that they cannot create a scene based on the CalArts community. This encourages the actors to leap away from what they know and to leap into their imaginations. It encourages them to discover and play out of their comfort zone.

Actors *must affirm their partner's impulses.* Now, that does not mean that if their partner moves into offensive or dangerous territory physically or emotionally that you have to go along with that. In recent years, much has been written about actors in improv groups taking advantage of scenes to harass or molest their oftentimes female-identifying scene partners. This rule does not apply to any behavior like that. Think of the old improv rule of "yes, and." It is very hard to have a scene in which the partner gives you a "gift" of place like, "Thank goodness you made it to the wedding in time!" and you as the partner respond with "This isn't a wedding." Rather the response should be something like, "Yes, and I'm having second thoughts." You want your response to be a "gift" to your partner and up the ante with an obstacle.

Actors *must include the position that they are in during the Space Rebound when "Scene!"* is called. It will inevitably lead some to begin an exercise class, but in time they will learn to expand their repertoire and see the many different possibilities. At some point I say that they cannot be in an exercise class.

Actors can be *anyone, anywhere, doing anything!* Giving this directive opens the performers up to conceiving all sorts of places, ages, locations, etc. As a stimulus, I will sometimes call out a genre like "Western!" "Soap opera!" or "Sci-Fi!" just before I say "Scene!" in order to demonstrate how different genres can feed their imaginations and conjure specificity in improvs. These genre scenes can be a challenging and fun way to find dynamic characters and situations. They can release all kinds of wackiness and vivacity into their bodies that feed the improvs. Of course they do not need to be funny, though often are. I encourage the students to work from the genuine impulses coming through, wherever they are taken.

It is so important to establish the following:

Who are you?
Where are you?
What do you want?
How do you get it?
What is your obstacle?

Listen carefully and build on what you get from your partner. Do not leave anything out. If it is introduced, it all has to be tied in during the improv. If an object is introduced in space, it cannot just be forgotten. Let's say you see a sword out of your Space Rebound position and begin the scene using the sword. The sword must not vanish in the next sentence. If you see it, the audience will. If it evaporates without explanation, we will be wondering where it went.

At first I call "Scene!" so all the scenes are happening simultaneously in the studio. This can get very loud, but it gives the actors a chance to work on their own before sharing for the entire group. They need a few of these rounds to get in the swing. I let the scenes go on for a few minutes, giving them enough time to find the answers to those essential questions of who, what, where, and the obstacle. The bell is used to get them all back to Space Rebound. It is important that they do this without comment and change on a dime back to that soft focus. This can be tricky with a wild comedic scene, but is great practice for shifting focus and concentration when needed.

Once in the scenes the actors need to commit fully to the circumstances they are creating together. Afterwards we talk about the discoveries, obstacles, "in the zone" feelings that emerged.

MARISSA: How was that? Observations?

GRACE: That was really fun.

MARISSA: What was fun about it?

GRACE: Well, I've always hated improvs but somehow, with this sequence, I found it easier to come up with things, it didn't feel as forced. Plus working with Joe is a blast.

JOE: Yeah, I like the flow we got in to.

MARISSA: Where did you start to feel that flow?

GRACE: At first in the mirror I felt uncomfortable. I realize I normally don't look people in the eye for long periods of time. But then we started to breathe together, and I honestly don't think either of us was leading after that initial awkward period.

JOE: I agree, it was a little spooky how lost in your eyes I got. We were moving together, kind of flowing together, and when Rebound came we were just in sync. Then Space Rebound took it to another level so when you called scene, I was in my body, not trying to be clever.

GRACE: Right away when you called Scene, Joe called me Eloise. Something shifted inside and I had to step into "Eloise." Suddenly I'm talking with a British accent and I'm an expert in horticulture. Where did that come from?

MARISSA: Your imagination. The whole sequence is designed to free you up, connect you with your bodies and your partner, to respond to each other and be ready for anything. I saw you both sliding on the floor at one point, shouting and totally committed to whatever set up you gifted each other with. It was a terrific example of what my teacher George Morrison called "go beyond the point of comfort." In order to create the reality of the circumstance you need to make full body commitment to that. Which means not hurting yourself but to "go beyond the point of comfort."

GRACE: That was the sci-fi genre improv where we were fleeing alien dragons on a broken-down spaceship while making a soufflé.

JOE: Yeah, I don't know how we got there but it was fun.

MARISSA: You got there through connection and trusting each other. That place when you are connected, breathing together, in sync, has a rhythm and it's the rhythm of you as partners at that very moment in time. You become present and leave behind your plans. That's where your gold is.

ANTHONY: Well I didn't feel free at all. I kept watching myself. Adzua was a great partner but I felt myself pushing us in to my ideas. I'm just so frustrated.

MARISSA: When in particular did you feel you were pushing?

ANTHONY: From the beginning, in Mirror.

MARISSA: What did you notice, sensorily, what was going on?

ANTHONY: I felt tight in my chest. I felt myself watching myself. I was clenching my toes.

MARISSA: Good, that's very specific language. Just bringing that to awareness will free you up more next time. Did you ever have fun, feel free?

ANTHONY: Yeah, there was this moment in Space Rebound when I let go. You said something about moving through molasses and I felt a kind of denseness in the air that I moved through. Also, there was a fun moment when Adzua became my mom in an improv and tickled me.

MARISSA: Take the sensory experience of that freedom and ground with that next time. The joy and connection you found in the tickle, and the Space Rebound molasses moment, are what to build on. Remember to apply awareness, without judgment. That's how we progress. Sensation is a key for you. Both the times you felt free were kinesthetic. Make sure that is your touchstone, feeling, sensing, everything else will fall in to place. It's the kinesthetic that brings you in to the present moment.

ADZUA: I saw that, when you released. When you laughed after I tickled you I heard your voice drop in. That's when you spoke without any hesitation and started gifting, giving me "yes and" for our scene.

MARISSA: Improvs can be terrifying, but if you can let go and trust that what you and your partner come up with in the moment will be infinitely more interesting than what you try to force of your own preconceived ideas, you'll be in that zone of abandon and play. Trust that. That's where your gold is.

I have watched students do this sequence for decades now, and I never tire of seeing how their imaginations open up. The sequence frees them to access that childlike playing space. That is one of the gifts of improv, the ability to play like a child again. The results are improvs that are grounded in the physical and take off when the partners truly give in to each other. Witnessing those moments when actors find story together in an instant in front of an audience is thrilling. We watch the actors in that rebound of inspiration. When it works, it is just great. When it fails, it is painful to watch no question. But more often than not audiences are forgiving if you just come back to the present and are honest about that. George Morrison used to say, "If you get stuck in an improv just stick your hand out and pull something new into the scene." What you need is all there, in the instant of discovery, in the eyes of your partner, in the space you share together.

7

WHAT PRO WRESTLERS TAUGHT ME ABOUT ACTING

I have had the good fortune to work with real-life superheroes as an acting coach for professional wrestlers at the NXT (next generation superstars), a professional wrestling television program produced by the World Wrestling Entertainment (WWE). Some of these wrestlers moved on to become WWE superstars. My work with these world-class athletes turned performers has led me to see firsthand the power and profound effect of the mythic and archetypal, and how those forces are incorporated in contemporary popular performance.

One day my husband came home after attending a leadership in professional sports conference, where he was on a panel that focused on working with high level talent. On our kitchen counter was a packet of images and stories of the up-and-coming NXT talent. They were people from all over the world with backgrounds ranging from the Olympics, professional sports, and of course professional wrestlers who had been playing matches on the independent circuit before being recruited by NXT. The profiles shared their passions and interests with an image of them in the spirit of their wrestling characters. I explored these pages and immediately felt a soul's pull. I recognized the archetypes they play with and felt a deep need to work with them. Archetypes are a central part of how I work with actors. I told my husband that day, "I have to work with these folks. I can help."

The next thing I know, I am on a plane to Orlando and meeting some of the most open, kind, gifted, and disciplined performers I have ever had the privilege of encountering. Before this, all I had known about professional wrestling came from visiting family in Miami as a child and curiously watching my cousin Alejandro passionately screaming at the TV while these huge men in crazy outfits toppled all over each other. Other than that, this was completely new terrain. I was welcomed respectfully and began leading workshops in gesture and archetypal work, as well as some acting basics. You have not lived until you have seen a 300+ pound professional wrestler moving gracefully in a gesture while accessing an archetype. It is a truly thrilling and tender thing to watch.

My time coaching these athletes and inhabiting their very unique universe has rocked my world and helped me find powerful allegories that have sustained me as an artist and person. They know they are performing in a story, in a fable of sorts, and they release an infectious energy in their audiences that is awe-inspiring. The more time I spend with these wrestlers, the more enamored I am of what they do.

What is played out between the characters in that ring, and off, is that classic struggle between good and evil. At times, the wrestler is at war with themselves or they switch from "baby" (good guy/gal) to "heel" (bad guy/gal). And all along the way the audience is on the journey with them, following the cues for how they should respond. The great wrestler is not only an incredible athlete, but they also know how to lead the crowd to follow their story. The crowd wants to know how to react; they are part of the drama and desperately want to be included. The better the wrestler, the clearer the signals to the audience for how they should participate; whether its chanting a theme phrase or miming a signature gesture, the great wrestler gets the audience to not only know their role but to play it with all they've got. And so, a dance emerges between wrestler, audience, and the hidden team that puts those elements together:

coaches, creatives, staff, announcers, etc. It is an incredibly theatrical experience.

I see this as an art form. It is part sport, part theater, part solo performance, part performance art, and a whole lot of drag. The drag part is connected to the way in which these characters are created from the extreme selves of the wrestlers. They externalize in dress and attitude their deepest Diva. They discover their power.

There is nothing fake about this work. It is as honest an art form as they come. When you see a wrestler flying into the air and landing on top of someone in the ring, they are actually doing that fully with their bodies and with precision and technical excellence. It is astounding. The wrestler is simultaneously holding their authentic and fictionalized selves at the same time and holding that mythic tension. And when it is done well, it is entrancing. It is a heightened version of the tension held between the actor and the character they are playing. Except with wrestlers the edge they play on is razor thin.

When working with wrestlers, I share a wide variety of archetypes and ask them to choose one or two that they are drawn to, that they feel is in the spirit of their character. All archetypes have a light aspect as well as a shadow. This allows the performer to access range and colors and move away from a one-note portrayal. We explore the light aspect of their archetype, whether their character is "heel" or "baby." The wrestler then invites that light side and embodies movement that comes from an inner knowledge of that essence. We then do the same thing with the shadow. The result is that the wrestler is given "permission" to step in fully and unapologetically to the energy and imagination that archetype affords us. What we may feel uncomfortable fully inhabiting is permitted through the light or shadow of the archetype. Details for character are found this way and can be used in the ring. Those are character signatures for them, and wrestlers can play with the same archetype and have very different results in the details found. It is a boundless resource.

A WWE wrestler I worked with, the amazing Tucker, looked as though a light bulb went off during one of our sessions. He described the process perfectly, saying, "You mean all I have to do is connect to the archetype and my bones will remember and I'll be that character?" I answered him, "Yes." It is a moment I have had the pleasure to witness many times. The archetype becomes the portal. The more open the wrestler/performer, the more the archetype comes through. This then leads to specificity of physicality and of speech, those details that draw an audience in.

When working alongside the coaches who do the seemingly impossible task of choreographing fight sequences when the audience fully surrounds the performers, I have often heard echoes between their work with the wrestlers and language we use for acting. In acting, the importance of "shifts" or "beat changes" is always discussed and implemented. This is what keeps the audience from "tuning out" or from being lulled and distracted because there are no surprises. It is the "shift" or "beat change" that wakes them up as they realize they do not know what is going to happen next. In wrestling the very same principle as it relates to the physicality is called "gear change." WWE shows are extraordinary in their ability to keep audiences engaged and the surprises coming. My work with wrestlers includes having them utilize that gear change principle for when they are speaking to the audience or on camera. The same gear shifts are needed to hold the audience's attention and draw them into your story. These kinesthetic performers get the principle right away. As one of the coaches said when we were working together, "We are about building moments." Whether in the ring or on stage or screen, the performer is building moments for the audience and taking them on a journey. These are moments that build to a pay-off and include surprises along the way. That is when we are doing our job well, for wrestlers and actors.

I have met with wrestlers in this process who struggle with finding their character. I have built a series of exercises to address this and help them mine their possibilities in a way that leads them to something they can be passionate about and is sustainable 24/7. These performers live their roles in public life constantly, and need to find ways to keep this fresh for themselves. They tell me that they are told to "just be themselves but amped up." Yet we are multifaceted, complex humans; we are all many in our one body. We have multiple personas in each of us and knowing what to bring forward and when is the challenge. It is one thing being yourself in your living room and another in front of 3,000 people. Any actor knows the challenge of "just being you." That is where the learned skills and resources come in, like archetype and gesture work, to help the artist find their needed anchors. If the passion for the character and the details of their inner life are not there, the portrayal is hollow. Once the connection is made to that inner passion and that mythic part of the performer, they take off and are captivating.

The dynamic wrestler Raquel Gonzalez comes from a wrestling lineage. In our work together, she connected to the power of that heritage and her Latina Tejana roots to forge a character that is both personal and mythic. The mythic acting tools help these performers find that balance, ignite their imaginations, and create a sustainable character with range and possibilities.

I realized through my work with wrestlers how important having tools for the inner mythic is in order to find that ultimate authenticity. It is really about connecting to what you love and giving yourself permission to follow that as you allow yourself to fully inhabit your part of the story that is unfolding. Every "heel" has an inner light side. Without a glimpse of that, they are unwatchable. Same with the "baby." No one is all good or all evil. Even the Marvel supervillain Thanos has his very slight glimmer of light.

Early on working at NXT, my son was diagnosed with a life-threatening autoimmune disease. This shook me like nothing else I had ever experienced. I steeled myself to be ready for anything my son needed. I am usually an emotional person but during this time I was cool and focused. A couple of months into treatments I was at a wrestling match and found myself in tears.

Belfast-born wrestler Killian Dain entered the ring with an electric ferocity that looked like he could decimate anything in his way. As he did this, I felt that power stirring in me to decimate the disease that invaded my son's body. I felt Dain become the embodiment of my inner struggle with this disease. I saw my son as a brave knight on a quest for health. I saw myself connecting deeply with Dain's unbridled power.

I see versions of this allegory being played out in the faces of the audiences. I particularly love seeing the little girls' faces light up when they see an example of power and grace through the women wrestlers doing an impossible move, or being nearly defeated then rising up miraculously to victory. Wrestlers like Raquel Gonzalez show that the athleticism of a woman on the ring is just as challenging and meaningful as their male counterparts. The little girls I see watching the shows see that in the same ring a Killian Dain dominates, so does a Raquel Gonzalez. The diversity of wrestlers I have had the honor to work with means that the audience is able to see versions of the rainbow around our cities right there in the ring. These are the wise tales of our time.

8

SOLO PERFORMANCE

Listening to Fate and Pursuing Our Destiny

It is no coincidence that the Goddess of the Arts is also the Goddess of Memory, Mnemosyne. That is our assignment: to remember. Not just our own stories, but to remember the vital stories of our culture.

In the storyteller and mythologist Michael Meade's beautiful book, *Fate and Destiny*, he offers an idea of fate that includes the potential for us to actively pursue our destiny. That destiny is linked to our *soul's purpose*. He posits that fate includes those things we were just born with: the parents that created us, our eye color and height, and all those small specifics that just came with our existence. Destiny is what we choose to do with those givens.

You must embrace fate in order to release yourself into your true destiny. I find this idea very empowering for actors and artists in general. Many of us find ourselves in the realm of the arts driven by some sorrow, despair, or a desperate need to alchemize traumatic experience. This view of fate embraces that the very same source of our pain is where our strength and purpose lie. Rather than re-write, explain, or distance ourselves from suffering, this idea has us move towards it, embrace it, and create work that moves beyond the personal. We traverse into the mythic, which is tied to the communal and age old. There is a great difference between feeling depressed and being visited by Saturn, the God of Melancholy and the Arts simultaneously. The mythic view of Saturn's visitation tells us that we are not alone in this visit; it has happened before and there are guideposts to follow. First, one is alone with one's state of despondency, then later one is part of a larger landscape in which visitations occur and we go through a ritual. These rituals have occurred throughout time and we place ourselves in the comforting fabric of the eternal.

Now, I want to clarify early on that by no means do I mean that depression or any mental challenge is not a serious issue for a person to face, or that medication should not be sought if needed. What I am offering is a way of seeing our condition that connects us to story and how people throughout time have faced challenges. We become less alone in our struggle.

While reading Meade's book I discovered that I was fated to be a member of a Cuban family who were exiled from their beloved country, while disillusioned with a revolution they fought hard for and risked their lives. It was my destiny to create out of the core energy of this nearly overwhelming disillusionment: I wrote and performed a play about that fate. In this example you can see how a potentially paralyzing event is transformed into a vehicle for self-expression, as well as education. While working on and performing this play, I felt connected to my soul's purpose. Yes, it began with the telling of a family story and my reflections growing up in this tempestuous Cuban American home; but the play also moved me to the ancestral, to the mythic theme of exile.

When I met Kalean Ung she was auditioning for the MFA acting program at CalArts, which I was leading at the time. During our conversation, she shared the idea she had of making a solo piece about her Cambodian father, Dr. Chinary Ung, an internationally renowned composer. Family members had shared stories about her relatives who were refugees from the Khmer Rouge/Cambodian Genocide. Right then I knew her story needed to be told and that our CalArts community could support her as she took this vision to reality. This began a years' long process in which she interviewed family members, took workshops, and sought council from CalArts faculty and friends. She teamed up with director and fellow classmate Marina McClure and created Letters From Home, originally work-shopped with Independent Shakespeare in Los Angeles.

During the process, Dr. Ung shared with his daughter letters he received while in the United States from family members in Cambodian refugee camps fighting for survival. The play weaves music composed by her father, those afore mentioned letters, songs, humorous family stories, and reflections on Cambodian genocide. Kalean is a master storyteller and she found a great balance between the lighthearted and hopeful sections and the necessary tales of this brutal war. At one point in Kalean's process she hit a dark period in the development. Kalean shared with me that she was having an emotional struggle with a section of her play. The pain in this particular part of her family story was unbearable. She did not know how to share it, yet she felt it was an important part to tell. "Find the metaphor, find the story," I told her. She then proceeded to meld a Cambodian fable with that of her aunt's tragic experience. Next is an excerpt from this section of the play.

Once upon a time there was a man and a woman with four hungry children. They were taken from the city and forced to live in a small hut near a river filled with crocodiles. But these were not ordinary crocodiles. These crocodiles wore black, had guns and they could stand tall on two feet. Everyday the man and woman and their four hungry children were ordered to work in the field and at night they would each get a small bowl of rice to eat.

After everyone fell asleep the crocodiles smoked cigarettes and played cards in the river, laughing horrendously. They guarded a mountain of books and if they caught you with one, they would drag you in the river and drown you. The man hid a book in his hut that he would read to his children at night before they fell asleep. But one day, the crocodiles found it and dragged the man into the river to never be seen again. So, the woman was left alone with her four, starving children.

The crocodiles punished the woman and her children and now gave them only one small bowl of rice to share. Each day in the field they would stand, point and scream at the woman and her children to work even harder. The children became hungrier and hungrier and she tried to comfort them by playing a game. She rolled a small handful of the rice into a ball and told them that a bird is flying over their heads and if they're lucky an egg would fall into their mouths. But each day the children begged the mother to feed them more and more rice. The woman realized that she couldn't keep all of them alive with this small bowl. She took the rice and rolled it up into many small handfuls. She looked at the baby. That night she chose to feed one mouth.

One day after all the books were burned, the river dried up and crocodiles moved out. The woman and her baby escaped through the jungle and into another land where women in white helped them to find their family.

A powerful way to tell something this challenging was through myth. Kalean found the universal metaphor which enabled her to connect her audience to a shared experience. She turned this horrific event of an impossible decision a mother had to make to feed one of her children over the others into a tale that gave voice to the insanity of that war. She found the craft that allowed us as an audience to hear, see, and feel that horror. The tale let us in, helped us to bear witness to a profoundly tragic event, and hopefully enabled us to learn from its lesson. By finding the crocodile metaphor, Kalean lifted her family story to the mythic, to those losses brought by war that fill us with empathy. It is a tremendously powerful moment in her play. Many members of the Cambodian community, as well as others who have tragically experienced similar events, told Kalean that the dramatizing of this story brought them healing and the ability to process for the first time.

Here, Kalean describes her mythic process:

In 2009 I had that seed but I wasn't ready yet to ask the right questions and go there. It took nearly a decade later, and a cultural reckoning within myself as an artist of why I MUST tell the story. I could not sit while I watched refugees being turned away from our country who have nowhere to go. Then the questions to family members came. This was the fate and destiny moment for me. I could not look away.

Often the culture does not want to remember, but orate the story we must. Sometimes the culture takes in a story as a woman dying of thirst takes a drink of water. So, get comfortable with digging for those tales within and around you. Right now, there is something stirring and you may not know why it is there. I had a character buzzing about me for two years, and it was not until I made the piece about her that the buzzing ceased. She was a Latina wardrobe-mistress of the Silent Era in LA who wakes up on a park bench on Olvera Street (the original center of Los Angeles) and the last thing she remembers was dancing at a Charleston competition at the Ambassador Hotel 80 years earlier. I learned so much working on this project about little known LA history. I think these stories come to us because they need to be told—and we are the vessels of their transmission. What we need to do is wait, listen, and be receptive. Much like the Contact Improv in Chapter 2, as writer-creators we need to attune ourselves to what is in the room.

> I just sit down and write, and I don't think. And the characters just do it. Sometimes they won't, and that's a bad day. . . . I assume if I keep myself open and don't take myself too seriously, they'll keep talking. I live for those unexpected moments. I don't really know when they will come out—I just know what I want to say. . . . Control so you can lose control—that's what writing is. Disciplined control. If you can sustain that for ten pages, you're lucky.
>
> —Eduardo Machado

Itzamná

Writing a solo piece can be a daunting task. I often see performers come to me with a glimmer of a story waiting to be told, only to find them shortly afterwards doubting the importance. Perhaps they are not quite ready to tell it, in which case holding off is wise. But I find more often than not it is the actor's doubts that prevent the story from fully coming into being, no matter how much I affirm that they have something vital to tell. We each have great stories inside us waiting to be brought forward. What we need is to develop the craft, discipline, heart, and courage to bring them forward. Oh yes, and the help of Itzamná.

Itzamná was the son of Hunab Ku and the Mayan God of Writing. Along with writing, he also brought humans healing, the calendar, and how to grow corn. He is often depicted as this really, really old toothless benevolent man holding a gourd, or perhaps an inkwell, and ready to hear anything you have to tell him. He is as compassionate as they get, which is what we need in the writing practice. We need patience, wisdom, and to allow our stories and our processes to evolve. If we get hung up on time we get stuck. Yes, writers have deadlines, but there is a saying I love and share with my students particularly when we are in rehearsal: "We don't have much time so let's go real slow." If we rush, we are bound to make huge mistakes and have to start over. If we take our time and follow our rhythms we will be right on track.

So, with Itzamná's help, his gentle wisdom and guidance, let us begin the process of creating a solo performance piece. You are encouraged to use any of our previous exercises, as many will be beneficial in this process. I often have playwrights in my classes and have seen many plays emerge from the Noir work, Sense Imagery, Life Study, and other exercises. These are pathways for acting work but also serve as portals into writing.

I have developed a road map to guide you along the way. As with all of my exercises and templates, feel free to adjust them to serve your needs. Follow your impulses and imagination with these prompts. I have outlined a personal process and later in the book offer a similar template for creating projects with an ensemble.

Before we move to the guiding instructions, we are going to do some stirring of ideas. Let us look to the Hindu God/Goddess Shiva as a portal. Shiva is known as the being that destroys evil, is a destroyer. They are often depicted split down the middle with Shiva on one side and the Goddess Parvati on the other: two beings in one. During the churning of the cosmos, a great poison that could destroy humans was released. In order to protect humanity Shiva drank the poison. The goddess Parvati stopped the poison from spreading and killing them by choking Shiva, making their neck and face turn blue. In our work we are always churning things up, and sometimes that churning has its consequences. Let us look to Shiva and Parvati for help here. Shiva is that part of us that can take the poison and keep it somewhere that protects us from its harm; Parvati has the good judgment to come to our aid when we need her and deflect the poison so it does not spread. There is an acknowledgement in this myth that we cannot avoid the destructive forces, but we can put a container around those forces and offer ourselves a way to transform with those experiences that leave their mark. The blue face of Shiva is a kind of scar. A scar is a wound that has healed, a remembrance of what has been overcome. There is great beauty in our scars. We can have gratitude for those marks of survival, but we need not let them define us.

Inviting Your Story to Come Forth

Just as with the Oracle Exercise, feel free to ask for guidance from any of the mythic figures that you are drawn to. Maybe you met that particular mythic figure through this book, or it is one you have long been interested in. Pay attention. Feel your way back. Take some time to think of a story that speaks to you, maybe has always spoken to you. Perhaps there is an old story you vaguely remember your grandmother telling you. This may take some research but I love to start my solo workshops with listening to a story from your family or culture that keeps returning. Many times, in my work with actors, when we begin this part of the process, they tell me about a song or story. It seems there is almost always a grandmother as the driving force of the piece they are working on. Listen to the grandmothers. I never knew mine in life, but they have guided every project I have worked on.

Once you have found that story take some time to reflect on it. The story will carry you. I suggest you use it as the arc of your piece, whether as inspiration or a structure you can lean on.

Beginning Prompts

Take out your journal and allow yourself to write stream of consciousness to the following questions:

What captured your imagination growing up?
Who were the people spoken of in your home?
What events happened that have stayed with you?
What people did you encounter in life or in stories that continue to come to mind for you?

Now write stream of consciousness on a couple of these answers that emerged.

The next step is to follow the following directions.

Research and Interviews

Once you open the research and interview doors, the floodgates open. You will be surprised by how receptive family members and others are about being interviewed. It is an opportunity for them to share milestones in their lives and can be a wonderful bonding process, especially for those elders who often feel discarded by family and culture. There are those who find visiting the past too painful, but more often than not I have found people to be more than willing to share what they know.

When approaching people to interview it is important to be honest about what you are making. If you speak from genuine interest and passion you will have a better time getting the information you need. People can sense when they are being tricked into revealing something. It is best to have as many champions of your work as possible. Many actors, who write solo shows in which people they know are spoken about in the piece, let those people read a final draft before performing the project. Not everyone does this, but it is one way of getting any potential problems out in the open early on, rather than while you are presenting the work publicly. There are folks who are sued by disgruntled parties who do not like the way they are depicted in solo projects. But that happens rarely.

Make sure you are researching from reliable sources. Enlist the help of librarians and, if possible, a student intern who is studying your subject/ themes. The archeological process of researching a solo piece can be a tremendously empowering and eye-opening experience. Those who seek out history, particularly those histories lost or forgotten, are aided by the ancestors needing those stories to come forward. Stay receptive to those voices.

River of Life Timeline

Every being is a building with music—grace upon grace upon grace.
—Carl Hancock Rux

Write your life as a timeline. If doing a solo show about another individual, you can create the same timeline using the following steps after researching and allow your embodied imagination to fill in what you do not know.

Take a piece of paper and make a squiggly line from the bottom left corner to the top right, like a river across the page. The furthest bottom left point is your birth; the top right point is today. Make five to six slash marks along the timeline that represent pivotal moments in your life, or, if working with another subject, pivotal moments in their life. Those moments that changed you and had tremendous influence (for example, the birth of my sister, the car accident, meeting _____, the death of _____, etc.). Write on index cards a short description of each pivotal moment. This same exercise can be done with fictional characters in order to bring details to their lives. Write about each pivotal moment and let the pen move along the page. Think freely and allow the memories to take you.

Now add to those pivotal moments smaller ones that are coming up as you work on this. You are creating a timeline of your life (or the subject of your solo piece), which weaves with the stories of those who have crossed your path.

Choose from your timeline an event, family story, person in your life, or a person that you have read about/been told about as your subject.

Investigate the subject by researching and interviewing knowledgeable sources.

One at a time, step into a character from the investigations earlier and imagine them in a particular circumstance. Improvise your text. Record yourself as you do. Then transcribe that recording. Pull what feels strongest in your storytelling.

Create headlines on index cards or Post-its for each section you've improvised/written. Let it be a rough draft. You are generating material. You can edit later. Put it all out there.

Inspiration Wall

Find a wall and paste onto it the following: names, images, quotes, thoughts, books, articles, etc.

Look at the wall of inspiration and let it guide you. Find connections. Group connections together on the wall.

Let the story of those connections speak to you. What do you see, hear, and feel as you put the pieces of the wall together?

Index Cards/Post-Its Map

Get index cards or colorful Post-its and write down the connections and potential individual sequences in your performance (i.e. the time I discovered an old family photograph and asked my father who those people were). Think of each index card as a kind of headline for that particular sequence. You can do the same thing with image- or movement-based inspiration. On the index card draw or paste an image you might use as a projection, prop, choreography, or scenery in that section.

Begin to play with each sequence on your feet, in a studio, or room large enough for you to move around in. How can you embody the content of each of these cards? If it is a text-based section then sit and begin to write that sequence. Allow yourself to find the text through conversation, improv, or poetry form. Play around until you find the tone that feels right for what you have written on the card. You may need to embody different people in this particular story to find out which voice can tell it the best. You may need to record yourself, transcribe it later, and then edit. Do this process for all your cards.

By now the index cards have turned to pages of material. Order the index cards in a sequence that feels like a good arc for the piece. Allow for surprises, twists, and turns. Be sure to follow the old writing adage: show, don't tell. Find ways to show through action the story of these cards, rather than just narrating. Become the child raising her hand in her third grade classroom and asking the question that set your life on its course instead of just telling us about it. Whenever you can, place us there in the moment. We want to go through what you went through, seeing/feeling/hearing what you saw/felt/heard. Configure the index cards as a map of your performance piece and place them on the wall.

Now look at your timeline, the wall of inspiration, and the map of your performance. You now can work from this structure. It may change completely but it is a place to start. "There is freedom in structure"—lots of people have said that and I can attest. Even the most experimental of pieces I have worked on have a very clear structure for us to play within, and it is that structure and container that allows us to fly. You now have a draft of your project. Now go play.

Let yourself move from improvising, to the wall of inspiration, to the index cards with headlines, seeing what develops for you. Where are Itzamná, Mnemosyne, Shiva, Parvati, and others leading you? Listen.

Try It Out

Many solo performers "test" their stories on family and friends through casual conversation. The great actress and solo performer Charlayne Woodard does this. I remember attending one of her solo shows and recognizing a story she had told me over lunch one day. I realized that during our luncheon she was gauging my reaction to see how it might work in front of an audience. This is a good idea. You can also do a version of this more formally for a group of people to get feedback on the work. When I was working on my solo piece, I had my director Mirah Love and my dramaturg Anne Garcia Romero constantly shooting me questions to clarify the text. I knew the stories inside and out, but chances are that if they had questions, so would my audience.

It is also important to choose folks who will respond to your work on its own terms. The playwright and Academy Award screenwriting nominee José Rivera is a master at offering feedback by picking up what the writer is attempting, and offering guidance on making that clearer in the storytelling. He does not offer feedback based on how he would structure that particular story. It is a tricky balance but an important one. If you are a movement-based performer, it may be best to seek guidance from people who do work similar to you; the same goes for text-based performers, visual theater artists, etc. Gravitate to those writers and performers whose work you admire and respect and have them share their thoughts on your piece. People are more receptive to helping out artists than you realize. The best advisors are those who are making work similar to what you are striving for. If the aesthetic is radically different, they may still be of help, or they will inadvertently want you to do something closer to what they are used to. I find this is particularly hard with creators doing interdisciplinary work. People will often look at the work and want to place it in one category, when what you are seeking is a fusion of disciplines. Also, seek out trusted family and friends outside of the field to give you constructive feedback. It is important to get the view from non-artists as well.

Here are a few things to share with your small team of advisors before you present the work. You may want to email them this list ahead of time so they are aware of how to be of help to you.

> Let them know the stage you are in for the creation of this project.
>
> Tell them what you are going for/seeking in the making of this work. You may want to be specific and ask for what feedback you need for different sequences in the project.
>
> Share with them how they can be of help to you. Perhaps you have specific things you want them to look out for. Make sure what you are asking for is clear.

Having clarity with what you need keeps the entire process healthy and the poisons out of the equation. You should also be sure to check in with yourself and share the work only when you are ready. This can be tricky when there is a deadline looming, but as best you can, put the work forward when you are ready to hear what people think.

When having a writing breakdown several years ago, my husband shared with me a wonderful lesson. I was crying after receiving what I thought was very harsh criticism for some writing I had done. He pulled out a copy he had of T.S. Elliot's *The Wasteland* that included Ezra Pounds initial notes on the first draft. The poem we know by that title begins two and a half pages into what T.S. Elliot wrote! And there were red marks all over the pages! This let me know that I had better get used to criticism. I would be in good company after all.

What is most important is that you allow yourself the time you need to let the project develop and take form. Do not worry how your friend did their solo show; that is not yours. Be open-minded and keep listening to your guides, those internal and out in your waking life. It is a tremendous honor to share your stories with others in this way. It was certainly the highlight of my creative life when I performed my solo show. I had never been more frightened and empowered at the same time.

Be sure to go back and forth between writer hat and performer. At least that worked for me and works for many I know. There are no doubt times you need to just sit down and write, others when you have to stop shifting text and learn what you have. But you will see that going back and forth will help inform both parts of what you are engaging.

The ability to hold the stage and share the story you brought into being with others can be transformative for a performer. Always remember to acknowledge those who helped you get there. Once performing the piece, remember also to acknowledge those who came before you, those whose stories you are sharing. You will feel their presence and guidance on stage when you need them. Although you may be out there seemingly by yourself, you are truly held by their helping hands, and they've got your back.

9

ARTISTIC VISIONING

Finding Home, Finding Tribe

In order to sustain your practice you must find nourishment, which means taking care of yourself. When you take care of yourself as an artist you commit to longevity in your craft and lay the groundwork for the demands of a creative life. Knowing what feeds your soul, what inspires you, what gives you sustenance, is of the utmost importance. You need to know what you are passionate about and to cultivate a community who will support those passions. You must activate your intuition, trusting in your instincts and impulses to lead the way. You must listen to all that is around you. I like to call the process of finding this individual nourishment, going to the well. Each artist must find the resources they need to draw strength and fortitude. That is your well.

Our life is a creative endeavor. We can craft a life from our innermost promptings and fashion it in a way that honors that soul. Within us is a multitude of expressions and creations waiting to be manifested. We are creating, whether we are artists or not, a way of life. If we compart-mentalize parts of our life, we have the danger of having them at odds. If you see the entirety of your life as an artwork, you pay more attention to the whole of your life, giving power to what may seem small but is very enriching in your daily life. The work is everywhere—in the best sense. There are opportunities to enjoy and employ your creativity all day long, even in dreamtime. This is important for actors to know since we often only recognize our worth or think we are being creative when someone from the outside validates us with a job or award. The truth is no one can keep us from doing our work, just as no one can keep us from living the life we need to live.

What do you do each day that can be infused with the spirit of your creativity? I always love to see the different kinds of journals my students bring into class. They are all so vibrant and individual. Each one reflects something about their owner. One journal may be very simple and tattered (I call that *very loved*), while another may have stickers and an extravagantly crafted drawing on the front, and another leather bound with initials. What matters is that you see these objects as extensions of yourself, as part of your creativity. And that is true with how you wake up in the morning, how you start your day and encounter the world. This can be done your way; this can be part of your artistic fingerprint.

Many actors play with this idea through their clothing choices, the car they drive, or the way their home is decorated. Bringing those choices forward consciously, deliberately, is a way of owning your creativity and claiming your signature. When you do this you are in the mythic mind. The world opens up. You do not need to be on that assembly line behaving as everyone else, liking the styles or fads you are told by the media to like. Start to notice how other people are creatively expressing who they are in their daily lives. In a way, friendships come right out of this matching of creative expressions and leanings.

It is too easy to see others in our profession as potential threats or competition. Taking the mythic holistic view, the one who sees another's creativity as part of a collective fabric we are building together, is the one who knows there is room enough for all ideas and expressions. There cannot be too many stars in the sky. We each have something specific to contribute. We each, when working close to our thread, have a tremendous amount to offer. That is why we are here. I do not have two students who want exactly the same thing, thank goodness! We each have specific stories to tell and work to make. How are those stories stirring in you? How can you find daily connection and expression to those stories?

What is stirring in you? What is calling you? Perhaps you have the desire to take a path, take a class, travel to another country, find a workshop, etc. and perhaps following through with that idea does not make any sense to you, but something in you says you must. If you follow through, that is *answering the call*. To me, a clear way of knowing I am following my inner-voice is when a feeling in my gut says, "I *am home*."

One day as a young acting student at SUNY Purchase, I went to the Neuberger Museum on campus. I will never forget the moment I entered that space. An artist's work was being presented who navigated and created in both the theater and visual arts worlds. I was 19 and had never heard of the artist before. Walking into the space I felt a profound sense that I was somewhere familiar, and the work stirred not only my heart but also my soul. Two human sculptural figures stood facing each other in an eerily mundane way, yet the distance between them betrayed a much greater distance. The air was filled with a stunning austerity. The pinpoint shafts of light led me to a feeling of church like reverence and mystery. It was a combination of theater and visual art, a new concept that immediately thrilled me to be witnessing. That artist was Robert Wilson, and many years later I lived a dream by performing in his production of *Danton's Death* at the Alley Theater in Houston. To answer the call one needs to be aware of those soul messages, know when we are in the presence of aesthetic family, and be ready to follow the lead. In spite of all the obstacles you move forward, move mountains, and live your dream.

I have developed this series of exercises through being a part of different strategic planning groups, both in the arts and in an elementary charter school I helped found. I have put together the exercise I found the most helpful in diving in and crystallizing one's artistic purpose. A group or company wishing to clarify their collective purpose can also do this exercise. There is fluidity to this work. Nothing is stagnant here. A week, month, or year later you may have very different ideas. These exercises are meant to help you clarify the direction of your passions at this moment in time. Yearly check-ins are recommended as things shift. It is important to revisit that vision you set forward and meditate on how things are going.

An Artist's Terminology

Here is some important terminology for artists. You will encounter these terms when applying for grants and in your overall training. The explanation of each is how I have experienced the way they operate within the artist's profession. Understanding them on a personal level can help us align with purpose and feel empowered in our process.

Vision—*How you see your life and work, what you value and the direction you are taking, why you do what you do and who you do it for.*

Mission—*A one- to three-sentence encapsulation of what you are striving for as an artist and person.*

Artist Statement—*Combines the preceding and goes in to detail about what motivates you, how your history feeds that, and your overall goals.*

For the exercises listed next you will need pen and paper, as well as different colored Post-its. You can get as creative as you like with these. Use different colored markers, paints; find a wall to take over and cover it with drawing paper. Be free to work in a large space if you can. Let your imagination lead you. Or keep it simple. Whatever feels right for you!

Grounding Exercise

Center and ground yourself. Listen closely to your deepest self.

Free write two minutes stream of consciousness on a piece of paper—

What I want is . . .

Now free write another two minutes—

*What I **really** want is . . .*

Then two minutes—

What I **offer** *is . . .*

Now look over what you have written. Let the writing "speak" to you. Circle any words that jump out at you. What are those operative words, those essentials you are seeing in what you have written?

Values Exercise

Take a moment to think about the following questions:

What are the most important things in your life and why?
What artists, living or dead, do you admire and why?
Who is your tribe?
What qualities do you admire in others?
If money were no object what would you be doing / what would you do?
If you had six months to live what would you do with your time?

This exercise will help you clarify your vision and inform your mission, artist statement, and ultimately your visioning plan. Do your own version of this, let loose your imagination, and make it yours.

Write out on a piece of paper things you value and are striving for in your art and life. Perhaps some of the writing earlier has helped you get in touch with those values. This is a time to allow yourself to connect with all the things that give you joy and that matter most in your life. Write them down. Use a timer and write for five minutes.

After the five minutes, take elements from what you wrote and write them on Post-its. Use the different color Post-its to help you categorize the different values and make groupings. The Post-its can contain single words like: family, ocean, basketball, dancing, etc. They can also be phrases: "Making work that is socially relevant," "Getting people to laugh," etc. Look at your Post-its and categorize them in whichever way seems right to you. Lay them out and find commonalities as well as when different areas overlap. Look and see what these groupings are saying to you.

Many of us inherit values that are not necessarily our own. This exercise makes space for honest reflection and guides us to our inner vision and wisdom. Only you know what is meaningful to you. No one can tell you that. Taking the time for this is paramount. Once you have clarity about your values you can begin to write your mission and vision statements. This will help you in making decisions as to how to best spend your time. We cannot be everything for everyone, although most actors wish they could. Having your mission/vision close and clear will make saying no to projects that do not serve that vision all the easier.

Goal Planning Exercise

Now that you have connected to your mission and vision and brought forward those values most dear to you, you are ready to set goals and create action items for achieving those goals. Write out three to five goals for six months, for one year, and for three years from now. Be sure to stay in the zone of proximal achievement. That means that the goals may be lofty, but attainable nonetheless. Share these goals with three trusted allies who can gently and with kindness hold you accountable. Write a list of people who can help you achieve the goals and create specific steps towards making those goals a reality. The seeds you plant today can make those dreams a reality tomorrow. Perhaps there are mentors, teachers, family friends, etc. who can be of aid. Perhaps you can reach out to those you do not know but whose work aligns with what you are seeking. Check in with yourself and this list every couple of weeks. Perhaps you will discover there are skills you need to expand on in order to achieve some of your goals. Pursue those skills. Your work from the exercises in this section will reveal much and, most importantly, bring into focus your true heart's desire. Anything that does not support that can go on the back burner.

Going to the Well

Our well is our place of nourishment. We keep revisiting our well on the journey to help us refocus. Our well helps us find our balance, our inspiration. Asking yourself these questions and journaling about them can help you realign.

What are the things that give you joy?
What are the things that inspire you?
What are the things that energize you?
What are the things that relax you and give you sanctuary?
What are the things that empower you?

When we know what our particular calling is, although it can twist, turn, and change shape like a river, we align with the purpose that stirs our souls. Saying no to things that take us away from that purpose, or yes to the right projects, is the key.

I leave you with a final message to sustain you on your actor's journey—

You are daughters, sons, and beings of Elegua, Lailah, Kuan Yin, Shiva, Parvati, Itzamná, Mnemosyne, and many others; those who have carried and inspired our stories for over 40,000 years.

You are agents of creation.

You are channels for the eternal.

You are imagination sowers.

You are myth and storytellers.

You make manifest fables and forgotten histories.

You challenge us to remember our true selves.

You breathe life into your audiences and help us to heal.

You inspire us to see, feel, and hear what we have been avoiding.

You bring us back to our sacred, soulful selves.

You crack open our hearts and suspend us in hopeful longing for your next word, your next gesture, your next thought.

You make us laugh and cry.

You make us scream the screams we wish we could make, sing the songs we wish we could vocalize, and dance the dances our bodies long to express.

You are artivists, shape shifters, fools, lovers, wise council, tricksters, and heroes.

You are storytellers.

You are mythic.

You are actors.

APPENDIX

Chair Exercise

The Chair Exercise allows us to explore the multiplicity of options for interactions with our bodies and the space and objects available to us.

I like to use this exercise when beginning the Noir work, but it can be used for any scene. The purpose is to get you to incorporate expressive physicality in your performance discovered through improv movement. Often actors have this expressivity in exercises and as soon as they hold text in their hands, their bodies go lifeless. Even in complete stillness we can remain alive in our bodies. The following exercises help you to explore that.

Chair Exercise Alone

Sit in a chair and go through the centering exercise from Chapter 2. Make sure you have a sturdy chair, preferably without arms. As with all exercises, keep that safe space but move bravely and with abandon. Now open your eyes and play with all the things you can do with your chair. The most obvious is to sit on it, but what other possibilities are there? Set the timer for 15 minutes of exploration. That is a very long time. You may find yourself running out of ideas. Just keep playing with the chair. Be sure to be safe with yourself and not attempt to do anything dangerous.

By now you will have discovered that there are a tremendous amount of possibilities with this one object. And yet, when we use a chair in a scene we generally do just one thing with it. This exercise lets you know that the exploration you tapped into with the chair can be used with every object you use as an actor, with the space, with the other actors, and with the text.

Chair Exercise With a Partner

Set the timer for ten minutes. Now you and your partner will face each other sitting on your chairs respectively. Do the exercise again and allow yourselves to play together with the same exploration. Perhaps the chairs come together in some way? Perhaps you crawl through the chairs together, etc. Let the body lead and be safe with yourself and each other. When the timer goes off, continue the exercise using the text of the scene. Be sure to move only when it feels right or to accentuate a shift in the text. Allow the chairs to be an extension of your words. Perhaps at the end of a thought you stand on top of the chair, or slink down underneath. Let the body lead once again. Free yourself of needing to make sense with this exercise. You are just playing after all. Find a good balance between the stillness and moving.

At the end of the text, start the scene again, then a third time. Write down in your journal anything you found from the exercise. Be sure to include any moves with the chair or moments of stillness where you felt particularly connected to your partner and the material. The next time you do the scene, see if you can incorporate some of the moves as staging.

Often actors feel at a loss when it comes to what to do with their bodies when acting. This is one way to find a focus that frees you from that kind of self-consciousness and helps you discover the power of using objects effectively. Look at actors who are masters at stillness. What happens is that they are so focused physically and emotionally that they let us in. Their thoughts are tangible and that brings us even closer to them. If you are thinking about how nervous you are or that ham sandwich you left half eaten in the green room, the audience will pick up on your distraction. All you need to do is be fully present, know what you want, know why you are there, and be responsive to your partners. Everything else is extraneous.

Image Board

The Image Board uses the power of imagery to inform character details and ignite the imagination.

Find a wall in your room or create a board where you can place images for your character/script/project that you are working on. Place it somewhere that you can see it every day. Start off with a couple of images and let it grow during your process. Take time each day to look at it and let the images speak to you. Write stream of consciousness as you look at the images. Use a timer so you do not get too lost. See how the image board can feed your process. Move to it one day, speak your text to it another. Change it around if it is not giving you anything or what you need. I often use a collective image board with my students for a particular project we are working on. The right visual inspiration can be a key for many actors.

Gesture Work

In Gesture Work, the actor investigates the power of gesture to lead us to emotion. In preparation for this exercise choose images of figures in painting, sculpture, and photography that have a specific gesture you are drawn to. Find images that incorporate the whole body and evoke a specific emotion when you look at it. You may want to find these images by going to a museum and being in the presence of the painting, sculpture, or photograph.

Put on instrumental music, something you may listen to in a yoga class or relaxing location. Look at the image you have chosen to work with. Have the image nearby so that as you explore you can reference easily. Stand in a neutral position and center yourself as you have in our previous exercises. Begin to allow the gesture in the image to take over. Move as slowly as you can into that gesture, feeling what moving into the gesture evokes, nice and easy. Take this in slow motion. The process of arriving at the gesture is what is most important, not the actual arrival. Begin to allow yourself to feel how the gesture, or moving into the gesture, evokes emotion. The gesture itself carries a history that you can tap in to in order to access emotion. Once you arrive at the gesture breathe into it, stay still, and dive deep into what the gesture is offering. If you like, in a voiced whisper with no need to project, begin some lines of text. Let the gesture inform your words, give in. When ready, release and move on to another image and gesture.

This has been a very fruitful pathway to emotional release and specificity. The action of putting my head into my hand and sinking low will immediately give me a feeling of loss or despair. We can use these gestures to open our channel and find emotional depth.

Life Study

Life Study is where the actor observes someone out in the world for an extended period of time. The idea of status is introduced. This exercise offers us the opportunity to have empathy for our characters, see the world through their eyes without judgment. When done in a group, we discover how status is a powerful storytelling tool that our bodies carry.

Find someone in the outside world who you are able to safely study for a period of time, at least ten minutes. This should be a stranger and done in a way that is not threatening to the person being observed. Watching someone at a bus stop, at a restaurant, in a library, etc. is the safest choice for observing. Pick someone who is very different from you physically. Watch them as they move, speak (if they do). Where is their center of gravity? What is the quality of their movement? Do they carry a certain pathos in their body? Do they move in a particular rhythm? Notice all the details you can about your Life Study.

Once you have done that it is time to step into that body. Close your eyes and center as in previous exercises. Bring to mind your Life Study and see them, eyes still closed, in front of you. Bring back all those details you observed. Now focus on the face. What is their expression? What are the details of that face? Lift your arms slowly in front of you and begin to make a mask, molding the air in front of you, shaping it in to the face of your Life Study. Don't make the mask on your face, hold your arms away from you and create the mask, eyes closed, in the space in front of you. Start with the shape of the head and then work in all the details, the eye sockets, the temple, the lips, the cheeks, etc. Once you have made the mask be sure to add the expression.

Now turn the mask around and slowly place it on your face, molding your features to the mask you have made. Let the rest of the body follow. Notice any feelings that arise as you step into this person. Slowly open your eyes and take in the room, seeing through these eyes, through this character. This section is done non-verbally. Come to standing and explore the room, notice what you are drawn to and repelled by. If you are doing this in a group notice how you interact with others. How do you feel in this space?

When ready you can go back to your chair and write in your journal. Be sure to have a ritual of disengagement beforehand. Stretch out if you were carrying a body with a lot of tension. Be sure to let it all go. Alternatively you can move on next to the following exercise.

Life Study Improv

In the Life Study Improv, the instructor leading the exercise tells the actors they are being held for questioning.

The instructor says the following: Behind this wall are the authorities. In a few minutes each person in this room will address them. You will answer these three questions—

What is your full name?
Where are you from?
Why do you think you have been brought here for questioning?

In the meantime, talk amongst yourselves. On the other side of the room there are donuts and coffee.

The actors improvise as their Life Study characters, interacting with others or not, depending on how their Life Study would behave in these circumstances. At some point in the improv they will be called to answer the preceding questions one at a time. They then will be "released" and can let go of the Life Study and write what they discovered.

This is a wonderful tool for finding character specifics and moving away from the habitual. Many of the actors I work with feel greater empathy for the person they observed after stepping into their bodies. This can be done as a source for creating a character for writing as well as finding a Life Study for a character you are working on.

Object Work

In Object Work, the actor brings in a found object, no larger than the palm of your hand, and relates to it. The found object must be "poor" and "worthless," something others would throw away or disregard, such as a gum-wrapper, bottle cap, shriveled leaf, etc. The object is chosen because its poverty is compelling to the actor.

Begin sitting in a chair with your journal and pen underneath the chair and the object on front of you on the floor and arms-length. Center and breathe. Step into the body of your character and continue the rest of the exercise as them. Connect with what your character loves most in the world. Maybe it is a person, place, idea, or thing, whatever the case may be allow for what first comes to mind. Let yourself fully connect to that feeling of that person, place, or thing, etc., that one thing that makes it all worthwhile, that you love above all else. Once you have fully connected to that, slowly open your eyes and see the object on the floor in front of you as the embodiment of that great love/passion/cherished thing. Slowly pick up the object and relate to it as if it were that great love. Discover its details and love it more and more. Take your time. Be with that object as the embodiment of what you love fully, whole heart, body, soul investment. Now see that object dying in your hands. It slowly loses its "life" in front of you. When it is gone place it somewhere in the room, laying it to rest and saying goodbye. Go back to your chair and write in your journal as the character with this recent loss for a few minutes. When done, let it go, release yourself from the character with a ritual of disengagement, and look over your writing. Notice what was revealed.

Through this exercise the actor infused the object with sacredness. They have now begun to realize the potential to transform and give power to the space they inhabit, their bodies, and the objects they are in contact with. If they can do that with a gum-wrapper they can do it with anything or anyone. This also brings us in to direct contact with what our characters cherish most and the specificity of what is at stake for them. How an actor interacts with objects is part of the storytelling. The way you pick up a pen that you got from the 99 cent store is very different than if it was your grandfather's who you loved dearly and before he passed away he gave it to you. The object itself will carry weight and storytelling if we interact with it with specificity.

Image Exercise

The Image Exercise is inspired by Bhutto workshops I have taken and the work of performer Dawn Saito. The actor embodies specific sensory imagery; a lightning bolt hits the body, a feather tickles the neck, the head is filled with helium, etc.; then these physical images are used to find "shifts" in text. This helps the actor to see the potential of vocal and physical shifts with the text as well as full body involvement. It is best to have someone lead this exercise, though it can be done on your own.

Stand in a neutral position and center as in previous exercises. Close your eyes and keep them closed. Imagine an ant is on your right temple and begins to cross your forehead towards your left temple. You can't swipe it away with your hand, but the rest of your body can react to that. Now there are ten ants, feel them crawling across your forehead. Now there are 20 and soon 100. Let the body fully react to that image.

Next, imagine that you are on a dry riverbed. Feel the dry earth beneath your feet. Maybe there are some rocks. Now there is a trickle of water that becomes high enough to get to your ankles. It is cold river water flowing at your feet. Feel the cold and let your body respond. Now the water is flowing and reaches your waist. How does the current affect your balance? Now your chest. Now you have to do all you can to keep your head above the water, to keep from being swept away by the current as the water gets higher and pulls you. Let that image go.

Now your head is filled with helium. Imagine your entire head is filled with helium. You might just float off if you are not careful. Give in to this floaty helium head feeling. Let it go.

I then have the actors take a monologue and divide it in to contrasting images for each thought change in the script. They choose whatever image they want to use but it needs to be able to affect the whole body and voice in a specific way, the way the preceding images do. So, one thought/section of text may be walking in to bright daylight after being in a pitch-black dark room, the next could be being tickled by a feather, another being struck by lightning, and so on. Now they connect with each image and add text, so the text is being informed by the image they have chosen. They need to take their time with this and make sure the image lands fully in their bodies before they speak. The actors then have very different and contrasting vocal and physical expressions coming through the text. It can be very liberating for performers, especially those who feel their personal lives are far from their characters, and have trouble creating a bridge between them. The image feeds the specificity. This is a powerful way to integrate body and text in an expressive way. It is great to do this exercise full out in body and voice, then to keep the images but use them subtly with stillness, just behind the eyes. When done correctly, the thought changes remain specific and the image helped us get there.

Duende Exercise

When beginning the Duende Exercise, the actors gather in a circle. One actor enters the center of the circle and begins a sound that can be repeated. She serves as "conductor" and begins to speak her text as she feels the Duende arise. She allows the sounds around her to feed her. She lets the outer circle participants to slow down, speed up, etc. to support her exploration. She releases in to the flow of the moment, allowing her voice and body to fully and freely express. With the help of others around her she finds a physical connection as well as the "music" of the text. The result is a communal supportive chant-like release. The results are always profound. It calls something ancient and tribal within us. I like to use sections from Federico Garcia Lorca's essays on "Duende" in order to prepare the way for this exercise. It is inspiring material that sets the stage for this powerful exercise.

INDEX

Note: Page locators in *italics* indicate a figure.